CAPTIVE

A Journey from Hell to Hope
The fascinating story of Bill Kropp

as told to
Sharon Garlock Spiegel

Amazing Things Press

Copyright © 2016 by Sharon Garlock Spiegel

All rights reserved. No part of this book may be transmitted or reproduced in any form by any means without written permission from the publisher.

Book design by Julie L. Casey

Back cover photo of child by Anna Garlock

Edited by David Paul Garlock, Jr., PhD.

ISBN 978-1945667190

Printed in the United States of America.

For more information, visit
www.amazingthingspress.com

"For God so loved the world that He gave His only begotten son, that whosoever believes in Him will not perish, but have everlasting life."
John 3:16

This book is dedicated to the memory of Bill's sister Suzie and his foxhole buddy, Shorty Mills. Both of them testified to him of the powerful love and mercy of Christ and His redeeming power. Both died before he experienced the saving power of Jesus, but he knows they are both in Heaven's grandstand where they have been "cheering him on" in his walk with the Savior.

Chapter One
Who in the World Am I?

My tears mingled with my blood, forming a pool at my feet. I couldn't control my sobs. They came in spasms as a little mud puddle formed, spreading its crimson river toward the porch where I sat. Accustomed to my adoptive mother's harsh words, the gusher of blood and tears was not from her verbal attack. At age nine, the whack of her broomstick on my head was common, but this time she had split my head open. I guess the blood sickened her, because that's when she locked me out of the house. The crisp November air cut through my light shirt and trousers. Usually I sucked in the hurt, both physical and emotional. That day I couldn't hold back the tears.

It was a way of life for me. I expected no less—but always wished for better. Maybe the day would come that I would hear sweet and loving words from my adoptive mother. Or perhaps a soft, tender touch. I'd seen her hold my sister Suzie, give her a kiss on the cheek, and draw her hand through Suzie's blonde curls, tucking them behind her ear. Hiding out of sight, I'd watch her caress little Suzie and tell her how much she loved her. Deep inside I ached with a hurt much worse even than the throbbing on my bloodied skull.

I was not jealous of Suzie; I knew she deserved those moments of "motherly" love, and I certainly did not. I was the "bad seed." It was the brand "Mother Kropp" gave me almost from the time of my birth. If there were tender moments between us, I could not recall any. The Kropps did not officially adopt me until I was five years old, but I'd lived with them from birth. As an infant, I assume I was properly fed and cared for. After all, I'd survived the critical first months and years every child faces.

Why hadn't my mother taken me to live with her? Why didn't anyone love me? Why was I born? These were the questions I would ask over and over from the time I had a conscious thought, throughout my pathetic formative years and beyond.

I was born, June 1, 1935, contrary to the date listed in my military record and on my birth certificate. You see, when the judge gave me the option of federal prison or the army, I lied and said I was seventeen. I was in fact sixteen and ran home to change my birth certificate to prove it to the judge. But I'm getting ahead of my story.

Who in the world is crazy enough at the age of sixteen to get himself accused of a federal crime and threatened with a long sentence in federal prison? Mind you, I was guilty. The year was 1951 and I didn't just break into the general store and steal penny candy, I managed to get into the cage used as the town's post office. Taking money from that office was a federal crime.

Excuses were a way of life inculcated by my mother from the moment of my birth. My mother, Margaret, was a homeless teenager. She found the best way to earn money was at a roadhouse in Lawrence, Indiana. It was strategically placed close to an army camp. Business was good for the young prostitute. I don't believe she knew who my father was, however, she told me once that he was an army captain. No doubt she was trying to do what she could to put my heritage—or lack thereof—in the best light.

Margaret's plight came to the attention of a registered nurse at the local hospital. With nowhere to go after delivering me, my mother readily accepted the generous offer of Mrs. Kropp to take us home with her. The Kropps then became foster parents to me and to my mother as well.

Margaret, however, was not content to settle down and be compliant with Mrs. Kropp's rules. My mother kept returning to the roadhouse and eventually had two other children, half-sister and half-brother to me. My half-sister Judy was with me at the Kropp's for a time but eventually went to live with our real mother, Margaret. I did not discover that I had a brother until much later in life. He was not around when I was very young. Whether Mrs. Kropps' disapproval of me was a retaliation against the rebellion of my biological mother or just an illogical hatred of me, I have no idea.

Living with the Kropp's would seem to be a better environment than Margaret could offer, which would have had me living on the street or at the roadhouse. However, if Margaret thought giving me up to the Kropps was going to insure a normal childhood with a mother's loving hand or whispered nursery rhymes at bedtime or ever being rocked to sleep, she was sadly mistaken. Why Mrs. Kropp wanted me as her son is beyond my comprehension.

From a very early age I was the object of Mrs. Kropp's mercurial outbursts. Our house—home seems a misnomer considering the torture I was subjected to there—was heated with steam radiators. On a whim or if I said or did something wrong, I was tied to the radiator and beat with a large, heavy broomstick. It was her tool of choice for punishing me. I say "for me" because none of the other children in the home received this form of punishment.

Mrs. Kropp learned that tying me there ensured hitting her mark, otherwise I would scurry away like a wounded animal trying to avoid the brutal assault. Splitting my head open and leaving permanent scars occurred more than once. My thick head of hair served to cover a multitude of her "sins." While the attacks were continual, I can't truthfully say at what age they began. Miraculously I did not suffer any broken bones. That is perhaps why the secret of what took place in our house went unnoticed by others.

Mr. Kropp, a mild-mannered fellow, was a baker and spent most of his time at his bakery. If he happened to be at home when Mrs. Kropp decided I needed a beating, she would hand him the broomstick and demand that he carry out the punishment. He devised a plan, making me a party to his deception. Jerking me by the arm he ceremoniously led me to a bedroom, loudly demanding I lie across the bed and take the consequence for my actions. He made sure his wife heard his command. He proceeded to slam the broomstick on the bed. My part of the charade was to howl every time he hit the bed. Although his plan rescued me many times—and perhaps saved my life—I still wonder why he did nothing to stop the abuse. He was aware of it. He, however, was not the head of his household. He would occasionally take me to the bakery. There was little a child my age could do there, but it was a relief to be free of the ever-present fear of a new and cruel punishment I might receive at the hands of his wife.

She no doubt caught on to his intention of offering me protection and soon put a stop to the increasing number of occasions Mr. Kropp was taking me out of the home. Her shrill voice pierced the air as I put on my jacket and slipped my hand into my adoptive father's large hand. His pores seemed engrained with the flour that was his trademark. I'd grown to enjoy the dusty scent of the white powder. Often, we were close to the front door when we were stopped cold by her voice.

"Where do you think you're taking the urchin?" Before another word was spoken, we were both aware that I wasn't going anywhere and that I would probably feel the impact of her anger as soon as Mr. Kropp disappeared out the door.

Just above a whisper, he dared respond, "I was just taking Billy to the Bakery to get him out from under foot." A fire-breathing dragon could not have fostered greater dread as she grabbed my hand from his. Jerking my jacket from off my back, she made me fall to the floor. She didn't even wait for the door to close behind her husband before kicking me aside.

The earliest abuse I can recall occurred somewhere around the age of three or four. Abusive incidents escalated from there. I don't know if I ever fully realized I was the victim of extreme abuse. All I knew was that I was treated differently than anyone else in the household and for no ostensible reason, I assumed I was a "bad seed" and deserved everything dished out to me.

It was a relief when I was locked outside the house and left for hours on the front porch even in the bitter cold of winter. As uncomfortable as this was, I preferred that punishment to powerful whacks against my skull. I was relegated to the porch most of the time where I would be sent without supper.

On more than one occasion, my brother Bob, a biological son of the Kropps, was able to sneak food to me. Though we were not blood related, I've always considered him a true brother. He was too young to do more to help me, but he did what he could and I knew he loved me. I don't believe I wasted time on feeling sorry for myself. Surviving each day, being able to make it through a twenty-four hour period without receiving a life-threatening injury, was how I counted the passing of time. The only time I would get a lump in my throat and come close to tears was when Bob did something that let me know he cared about me or when I'd see tears pool in little Suzie's blue eyes when I was being punished. Tears I shed then were more for their hurt than my own. At a very young age I became hardened to tears. I didn't want my "mother" to see me cry. Sometimes I would howl, however, from the intensity of the pain, but I learned to control the flow of tears.

The porch was also where I slept. The cold and fear kept me there all night and generally resulted in my wetting the bed. For this my punishment was worse than the beatings. I was shamed in front of my schoolmates. I was not allowed to change out of my wet clothes and was sent to school to be taunted. Being uncomfortable in my soiled things and smelling of urine increased my loathing of school. I could neither read nor write and learned nothing but how miserable a person's life could be. The humiliation and taunting by my classmates kept me aloof and made it impossible for me to form any friendships.

At the age of five, the Kropps became aware of a newborn baby girl named Suzie that was born with a serious defect—her bladder was outside her body. She required surgeries and special care. Her mother was told she would not live past age five. Again, because of her position at the hospital, Mrs. Kropp knew of the situation. She stepped up and offered to adopt Suzie, a tiny blue-eyed blonde in need of a nurse's expert care. The double adoption was a package deal: little Suzie, helpless and sweet and me, the five-year-old "Dennis-the-Menace" demon child.

To say I was unhappy is a severe understatement. Of course in order to understand "unhappy," I would first have had to discover what "happy" was. So it would be safe to say I was not unhappy, just miserable with no clue as to why I was even born.

I loved my little sister, Suzie. My older brother Bob continued to show me token acts of kindness. I don't think he was happy in the home. He joined the army as soon as he was old enough to do so. The Kropps had another biological child named Joanne. She was another little sister in my life.

Suzie was such a blessing in my unfortunate existence, I welcomed this second little creature and loved her immediately. While I adored her, I hated Mrs. Kropp. I felt no love for her and had no desire to please her. Perhaps that is why I worked so hard to upset her. So accustomed to her deviant forms of punishment, I didn't seem to have any control over misbehaving and receiving continued abuse. This was my life until at age eight, I found myself on the front porch, bleeding. I was convinced no one cared whether or not I died out there. How I wished I would die. The crazy thought came to me that maybe if I shook my head, all my blood would gush out and I would bleed to death. The only thing I accomplished was making my head hurt worse and I staggered up the porch steps to my cot where I curled up, pulling my ragged blanket around me. I cried myself to sleep while blood soaked my unwashed, fetid sheets.

I moved from one kind of trouble to another. Rejection was the prominent feeling overpowering me, with hatred my ruling emotion. The love and acceptance with which the other children in the house were treated served to punctuate my rejection more. To add another wound to my already tortured psyche, my biological mother, Margaret, came to the Kropps and said she was going to take my half-sister, Judy, but not me. Margaret had married and was trying to get some normalcy in her life. I took this as a personal blow—the ultimate rejection. At the time I did not realize because I was legally the adopted child of the Kropps, it was impossible for my mother to take me to live with her. They had never adopted Judy. The irony was, though I was adopted and legally a "Kropp," I felt no part of the family. I did not understand why Margaret didn't take me. Rather than give vent to the tears and anguish bottled up inside me, I lashed out with more bad behavior.

My brother Bob had a friend with a car. They both took the time to give me a little fun in my dismal life. Randy, Bob's friend, let me drive his car on a side road. Taking me along for some afternoon excitement, I think they got as much of a "kick" out of it as I did. How I enjoyed the time I spent with these older boys. Somehow Mrs. Kropp always managed to have an intuitive idea that I had experienced some fun. She would configure some way to accuse me of something that deserved an extreme punishment. After one such occasion where I was again tied to the hissing radiator close enough to suffer burns on my legs and received a severe beating by the broomstick, I decided I would run away from home.

Since Randy had let me drive his car, I felt confident I could drive far enough away that no one would come looking for me. One day when the car was parked outside our house, I slipped into it and stole it. I didn't care if I got caught; I felt power behind that wheel. I was on my way, away from the Kropp house, but I had no idea where I was going.

Obviously, I had not thought through my plan well at all. The problem was that at age nine I couldn't see over the steering wheel and ran into a tree. I tore up the car. I was graduating from mischief and devilry to real crime. Up until this time, fighting and stealing candy from the store was the extent of my criminal record. I don't know what had possessed me to steal the car of someone who'd been nice to me. The whole episode would be comical if it were not indicative of the direction my life was heading.

There was some good that resulted, however. Out of shear exasperation, the Kropps together decided to send me to live with my grandparents, Mrs. Kropp's parents.

Chapter Two
Grandpa's and Grandma's House

Grandpa Brown owned a dump and salvage yard. Arriving at their house, I was prepared for another bout of rejection and torture. After all, these were the parents of "Mother Kropp". Not knowing for sure what to expect, I was sure of one thing—this wouldn't be good. If Mrs. Kropp considered it a punishment to be banished to the grandparents' home, it had to be bad.

I was not prepared with how to cope with the love and acceptance I received from them.

Arriving in the late evening, Grandma shuffled me off to bed. For the first time I could remember, I slept in a room that was part of the house. The bed sheets smelled like fresh air in the summer and a thick quilt gave warmth I had seldom experienced. The situation was so foreign to me, I didn't know what to think. Waiting for a harsh comment, I was stunned as Grandma Brown tucked me in and said, "Sleep well, Billy Boy!" With a soft pat on my head she added, "We wake up with the chickens around here, Billy. So get a good night's sleep. Grandpa will want your help tomorrow."

With a quick peck on my forehead, she bounced out of the room. I had a lump in my throat. It was not because I was homesick.

Heaven's NO! A feeling I'd never experienced overwhelmed me. And I wept, dousing my pillow with tears. Then I fell asleep and dreamed about Grandma's soft hand on my head and her soft words. She called me *Billy Boy* instead of *idiot*, *stupid*, or worse, which I was used to being called.

Grandpa put me to work right away. I loved poring over the junk people brought him. He taught me what had value and what was useless. He promised me I could keep the profit from the scrap iron I saved. I was so excited as I carefully set aside my own little stockpile. He seemed to enjoy pointing out what was worth salvaging. As the days passed, I began accumulating a tidy little sum. I couldn't believe I was allowed to keep my savings.

I'd been paid small amounts when doing odd jobs in my prior "home." Bob and Randy got me a job as an usher at the local theater. They took me along when they worked as caddies and I would caddy with them. But my money was always taken from me by Mrs. Kropp who demanded I hand over the money I'd earned, reminding me of my worthlessness and the fact that I owed my existence to her and Mr. Kropp.

Receiving pay and being allowed to keep it was a new and exciting experience. And even more significantly, I actually enjoyed working beside my grandfather. He was strict and a tough boss, but he was fair. He took the time to teach me when I needed correction. My desire to please him brought a huge change in my behavior. The fact that there were no punishments meted out neither for minor missteps nor for "bad" behavior was a new concept of living for me.

Fall arrived and the leaves were changing to brilliant hues of red and orange. After working in the salvage yard all day, Grandpa put his arm around my shoulders.

"Son, I think we should go fishing after supper tonight, what do you say to that?"

I couldn't speak. No one had ever called me "son" and I had never been fishing. The lump in my throat was so big I couldn't swallow. Looking up into the old man's kind face, I nodded. It took all my strength to hold back the tears.

As we entered grandmother's kitchen, the smell of her famous apple pie set my mouth watering. She was an excellent cook. My scrawny frame was putting on weight with the delectable meals she prepared. With the excitement of the anticipation of going fishing, I wasn't hungry at all. Grandpa must have guessed my lack of appetite.

"Now, Billy, you clean your plate. Grandmother worked hard cutting up and frying all this chicken. You eat up, and eat a piece of that good pie too. Once you finish, we'll pack our fishing gear and head out for a night on the lake."

Grandma smiled at him. "Bring back some of that good crappy. It doesn't have that old muddy taste like catfish, and we'll have a good 'ole fish fry tomorrow night."

I managed to put away quite a bit of chicken, mashed potatoes, and green beans, as well as a good-sized piece of pie. I don't know which was fuller, my stomach or my heart. I was going fishing with my grandpa.

It was not the last time he took me fishing. Our evenings and sometimes early mornings on the riverbank were the best memories of my childhood. Most of the time there was little or no conversation. When he did speak, his voice was gentle; he made me feel important and a part of his life.

When business slowed at the salvage yard, he got me a job setting pins at the bowling alley. I was paid two cents a rack. It wasn't easy work for a young boy. I was ten then. Every rack I set, I tried to add in my mind how much money I was making.

My stash, which I kept under my bed at Grandma's, was growing. I had close to $30.00. I felt like a millionaire, and it had very little to do with the money I had saved.

For the first time in my existence, I felt cared for and even loved.

Winter hit hard that year. Shoveling snow made me a few more dollars. Most boys my age would be bored, cooped up with two older grandparents on cold snowy evenings.

I was delighted to enjoy the warmth of the hearth, watching Grandmother embroider her quilt top and Grandpa listening to Fibber McGee and Molly on the radio. Life was good. No broomstick torture, a real bedroom and soft bed to sleep on. It was all too good to last and it didn't.

The first indication that my life was about to change again was when Grandma had a stroke. There were no more delicious meals. That didn't bother me and I was happy to do everything I could to help her. She recovered some, but could no longer cook and clean. She spent most of her time sitting in a chair and staring out the window. My heart hurt for her, I could see the frustration in her face. Her speech was slurred and she was no longer the same person she'd been when I first came to their home.

Trying to keep the salvage yard going and taking care of Grandmother took its toil on Grandpa Brown. I'll never forget the day he sat down beside me and told me I would have to go back home.

Home, I wanted to scream. *This is home. This is the only home I've ever known. Please don't send me back there.* While the thought pulsed through my mind, I didn't have the nerve to say the words. Instead I tried to offer a solution.

"Grandpa, I can run the salvage yard for you and you can stay home and take care of Grandma. I can even cook some things; I can scramble eggs and boil potatoes."

I tried every argument I could think of. I felt like I was drowning. I couldn't go back to live at the Kropp house. It would be so much worse than before because I'd had a taste of what a real home was like, a home where I felt wanted, loved, safe. I just couldn't go back.

"Please, Grandpa, please let me stay, I can help; I'll do anything you ask me to. You can have the money I've saved."

It had been my last ditch effort. I thought if I contributed to the household needs, Grandpa would let me stay. Holding my meager savings out, I offered them to him.

"Here, Grandpa, take my money. It will help, won't it? You and Grandma can have it to get things you need. If you let me stay, I'll keep working and give you the money. I won't eat much; it won't cost you much to have me here. Please!"

I know he saw my desperation, but it was not practical for me to stay. And if anything, Grandpa Brown was a practical man. Even while I was trying to bargain for some way to stay, I knew it was futile.

"You keep your money, son. You earned every penny of that. It's yours. Grandma and I are getting older and we just can't let you stay. We may have to move to a smaller place. You go home, son. We've enjoyed having you here and we'll miss you, but you can't stay." Grandfather had a sad expression as he shook his head. My only consolation was that I knew he meant it when he said he would miss me. We'd had a good time together but it was over.

"You're just a lad, son. How old are you?"

"Eleven in two months," I said, gulping past the huge knot in my throat.

"I'm sorry, Billy. We've enjoyed having you here, and you're the best fishing buddy I've ever had, but it's time for you to go home. Grandma and I will just have to look after ourselves. We'll miss you. I'll make arrangements for someone to be with Grandma on Saturday and then I'll drive you on home."

"If you'll give me a chance, I could run the yard and work hard, make extra money for you and Grandma."

I didn't even try to hold the tears back. The rug was being pulled out from under me. My security, my happiness—it all evaporated with Grandpa's next words.

"You're too young. Now dry your tears. Pack your things up. You'll be glad to see your folks, your brother and sisters. You miss them, don't you?"

Holding in the words of hatred I still held for Mrs. Kropp, I nodded and tried to convince myself it would be good to see my siblings.

Saturday came. I was packed. The little pouch with my $37.00 was deep in the pocket of the new trousers Grandma Brown had made for me. I planned to squirrel it away in a suitable hiding place and somehow get enough money to run away if things didn't improve back at the Kropps.

With a hug for my ailing grandmother, I assumed a stiff upper lip and left the only placed where I'd felt at home. Grandpa sat erect at the wheel of his car. He never spoke a word on the long ride. I rested my head on the side window and feigned sleep. I couldn't' have responded if he started a conversation. I felt like a condemned man being led to the gallows.

Stopping outside the Kropps' wood-frame house, he turned and said, "Well, you're home, Billy. You've been a good chap for Grandma and me. We'll miss you, but this is where you belong."

His gray eyes filled with moisture and I turned away from his gaze. Jumping out of the vehicle, I bolted for the front door. I was not going to cry.

The next sound I heard was his vehicle's acceleration. He pulled away from the curb as I turned. With my hand on the doorknob, I stood watching until he disappeared down the road.

I could almost hear my hope of a welcome home shatter as Mrs. Kropp's voice erupted from inside the house.

"Don't just stand there like an idiot. Get inside and give me the money I know you must have earned at your grandfather's house. I know how the old man is. I imagine it will take me some time to knock some sense back into your head after being spoiled by your grandparents."

Chapter Three
Father Lloyd's Boys' Home

My return home was not a joyful celebration. Christmas was coming, but that was meaningless to me. I'll never forget my second day home. Forgetting to rinse off my supper dish was an egregious sin. It must have been, considering the punishment I received.

The familiar whack of the broomstick didn't hit its mark—my skull. I pulled back, receiving the force of my adoptive mother's swing on the bridge of my nose. Blood poured out in rhythm with my heartbeat. Mrs. Kropp picked me up by the nape of my neck and dragged me to the bathroom. A trail of blood splatter marked our path.

She ordered me to bend over the toilet; as I did so, the blood continued to gush. As a nurse, she should have known she'd broken my nose and a major blood vessel. She should also have been aware of the Crista Galli bone that separates the two frontal lobes of the brain. As an illiterate child I didn't have a clue that she'd come very close to killing me that day. Had her fierce hit pulverized the bone behind the bridge of my nose, she'd have become a murderer. As it was, the blood flowed uncontrollably.

"Keep your head down and over the stool." Her high-pitched command rang in my ears.

Coughing and gagging on blood, I tried to lift my head to answer her. She pushed me to my knees, forcing my head further into the toilet. Sure I was dying, I hoped I was.

Blood everywhere—the trail to the bathroom looked like someone had been slaughtered. Suzie started crying. Bob and Mr. Kropp were not at home. I believe I would have bled to death that day had Grandmother Kropp not burst through the front door. She'd unexpectedly stopped by for a visit. Hearing the commotion, she let herself in and headed to the kitchen. When she saw the blood spatters, she let out a scream and came to my rescue.

I'm not sure if she had a clue about the abuse I suffered, but she saved my life that day. Picking me up, she pressed a towel to my face, trying to stop the blood flow. The hurried trip to the doctor's office is a fuzzy memory. No one asked me what happened. My nose was packed, as Mother Kropp had broken it, and I was sent home.

I have no idea what my "mother" told the doctor or Grandmother about my injury. I've often wondered how she would have explained away my death.

The time I spent at Grandpa Brown's house in Ravenwood, Indiana had been an oasis in a barren desert. During that respite from abuse was also, no doubt, a lifesaver. Mrs. Kropp's attacks were escalating. My behavior worsened as well. The punishment sessions took me from one illegal caper to another.

The experience with the broken nose did not seem to faze her. The head-splitting attacks with the broomstick were many. Perhaps she realized how close I'd come to death when she struck me on the bridge of my nose and she considered me "hard-headed" enough that her whacks on my skull wouldn't kill me.

My antics took me finally to a place called *Father Lloyd's Boys' Home*. It was hoped they would "straighten me out." In retrospect I wonder if Mrs. Kropp was afraid she would kill me and sent me away to save my life. She had to know how out of control she was where I was concerned.

When I was told I was being sent to a boys' home, I was relieved. I wondered if I could possibly make some friends being around other boys my age. At this time, the Kropp's biological son, Bob, was in Baltimore, Maryland at army boot camp. With Bob away in the army, Suzie and Joanne were all that I missed about leaving the Kropp house. I was actually excited about the change of venue. What Mrs. Kropp considered a punishment, I looked forward to.

That is until I arrived. From the very first moment, I was treated as a criminal and relegated to a miserable existence. The food was awful and the treatment worse. I felt like I'd been thrown from the frying pan into the fire.

Most of the other boys in the place were delinquents. I was bullied by them as the "new kid." My idea about making friends was soon squashed. To say it was strict is an understatement. A sharp crack across the knuckles with a thick board was the answer for the least little infraction. That may seem like a small thing considering the punishments that I was accustomed to, however, for me it became the proverbial "last straw." I could take no more. I saw some of the smaller boys have their hands crippled as the board broke their fingers. The stout wooden paddle became my enemy. I'd had enough.

I devised a plan of escape. I was thirteen years old but still could not read or write, although the teachers at the school assumed I could. I would lie in bed at night and hear the whistle of the freight train passing nearby. My plan was to hop a train and head to Baltimore to join my brother Bob. He and Suzie were the only bright spots in my life. I was sure he'd take care of me.

They had us work long hours in the acres of Iowa corn fields surrounding the compound. There was a train track running along the edge of one of the fields. Maneuvering my way through the cornfield maze, I managed to place myself working in a spot close to the track. Each day I watched for an opportunity to jump on a passing train, not having a clue where it was headed or how I would survive on my own.

My first attempt failed. The train was moving too fast. No one in authority noticed me so I continued to worm my way close to the track as I worked, hoping my next try would be successful.

I was afraid someone would "rat me out" about my escape plan. I hadn't shared it with anyone, but one of the bigger bullies saw my failed attempt. I was sure that would be the end of my plan. Surprisingly he approached me that night after our meager supper of bean soup.

"I saw what you tried today, kid. You're doing it all wrong."

Ignoring him, I carried my soup bowl to the kitchen and put it with my silverware in the soaking tray.

"Hey, kid." The bully followed me as I left the dining room. "I can help you if you'd like. I'd try to hop a train with you, but I get to leave here next week when I turn sixteen."

My ears perked up at his offer to help. I knew I needed help, but also knew he could be setting me up. I let him catch up with me. Looking around, he kept talking.

"You have to be ready to hop the train when it slows down at the crossing, just a little ways away from the field we're working. You can't wait till it gets down where we are; that's when it picks up speed. You'll get killed if you fall under the wheels of that train."

Turning toward him, I asked. "So why are you helping me?"

"Because I think you've got spunk and I want to help you get out of here. Don't ask a lot of questions, just be happy to get some help."

He continued, "This is what you have to do: I'll be a look out for you and you can hide in the corn when you hear the train whistle. Work your way through the rows until you get past the field and toward the crossing. When you see the train, run for it. I'll cause a ruckus with one of the other boys to take their attention away from what you're doing."

I couldn't believe he was going to help me, but I nodded. "I'll give it a try. Thanks!"

"No problem. Good luck." He disappeared down the hall as one of the overseers appeared to my right.

"What are you up to, Kropp? Do you want to spend the night in the hole?"

"No sir," I was quick to respond. All I wanted to do was get out of this place. Without looking back, I headed to the ward where my cot was set up with twenty others. When I wasn't called back, I breathed a sigh of relief and headed to my bunk where I lay down, my head full of my escape plan.

I gave no thought to what Bob's circumstances would be at the boot camp. My limited knowledge didn't take into account he wouldn't be able to take his brother in while training. I assumed he'd be glad to see me and would take care of me. The year was 1948.

While my plan was not carefully thought through, I had asked one of the older boys if he knew which way Baltimore, Maryland was. My next step was to find out if the trains passing were headed East. I was smart enough to make my inquires general so no one would figure out my strategy. My new friend, whose name I did not know, was the final piece to my plan.

The sun was hot the day my plan came to fruition. I heard a distant whistle just before we were offered a short break when the water wagon pulled into the field. It was several yards from where I was working. As everyone gathered to get a drink, I slid on my belly through the tall ears of corn near the railroad track.

Hoping the approaching locomotive was eastbound, I slithered toward the rail. I calculated that even if I was spotted jumping on the train, there was sufficient distance between us that the person guarding could not get to me.

Spotting the train approaching, I crossed the track, putting another barrier between me and those supervising our work. I followed my fellow conspirator's advice, edging closer to the crossing and farther from the corn field. The train slowed as it approached.

The echoing sound of the locomotion and the train's whistle added to the excitement I felt. I was really going to do it this time. Spotting an open car, I ran alongside and with a spurt of adrenaline gave a leap, grabbing hold of the edge of the floor of the railcar. Hanging there, I held on for dear life. I felt the acceleration of the train as the engine picked up speed as it passed through the crossing.

I must have been a sight to those waiting for the train to pass, hanging there, not knowing how long I could keep my grip before I fell. Fear was something I didn't know. Having suffered so much physical and verbal abuse, nothing hindered me from taking chances. My mind was intent on getting into that car and I was going to hang on until I could hold on no longer. If my plan failed, at least I'd be away from the detention center and far away from the Kropp home. I'd be free—even if I died from the fall.

How much time passed as I hung suspended there, I don't know. It seemed an eternity but I'm sure it was only a few seconds at most. When I thought my fingers would be cut off from the pressure of the sharp edges of the moving freight car, I felt someone grab both my arms.

As I was pulled to safety inside the car, I was amazed to see my rescuers. There were two of them. They let me lie there on the floor to catch my breath. Then they introduced themselves as Jack the Hobo and Jim the Bum. I was not afraid of them—probably because they had just saved my life.

Laughing, they welcomed me to "their" car. When I regained my equilibrium, they offered me something to eat. I readily accepted the bread and cheese. They had quite a stash of food. The fruit was the most plentiful. Jack told me he was a professional hobo. I was intrigued by his stories. Producing a "business card," which I couldn't read anyway, he was proud of who he was.

They made me feel at home and didn't ask me a lot of questions. I told them I wanted to go to Baltimore. They said I'd made the right choice by hopping their train. We were headed east and would be stopping in Chicago, where they would help me get on another train going in the right direction.

So my adventure began. I'd never been happier, except for the time I spent with Grandma and Grandpa Brown. Jack and Jim treated me as an equal and showed me how to grab food along the way when the train made brief stops.

They shared their blankets with me, and the expertise they shared with me about living on the run was fascinating. I considered sticking with them and forgetting about Baltimore and my brother, Bob. While they watched over me and made sure I had plenty to eat and was kept safe, they discouraged me from taking on the life of a hobo.

When we pulled into the busy Chicago terminal, they insisted I stay in the car while they scouted out food sources and what train we should board next. I'm sure they altered their own itinerary to see me safely to my destination. I'd found the right train and the right men to help me.

After a switch of trains in Chicago, my journey continued with my new friends. As the locomotive rumbled down the tracks, headed toward Baltimore, they told me unbelievable tales of their lives before they became homeless bums, living on the rail. I'll never forget those fellas and the fact they watched over me as the miles ticked off until we pulled into the station in Baltimore.

The railroad yard was a bit overwhelming. There were groups of other hobos gathered around fires they'd built in metal drums. Jim and Jack told me to steer clear of them—they were up to no good.

I didn't have a clue as to how to find my brother. Jim and Jack took me to a public park near the railroad and told me goodbye. I felt important as they shook my hand and wished me luck. They handed me a sack with some fruit and a blanket.

"It's been a pleasure traveling with you, Bill." Jack patted me on the back as he wrapped the blanket around my shoulders.

"You might need this tonight if it gets chilly. Just as soon as you find someone to ask about finding your brother, do so. You don't want to hang around this park too long."

Looking around to be sure no one was listening, Jim said, "I don't suggest you ask a policeman. They might haul you in. Don't know why you ran away from home, but I'm guessing things weren't too good there, and they'll just send you on back."

Nodding, I thanked them for the food and blanket and watched them head back toward the rail station. There was a lump in my throat and I hesitated, wishing I could follow them. They'd made it clear that the life of a hobo was not for a child of thirteen.

Glancing around, I didn't see anyone that I felt comfortable asking for directions to the army camp. Sitting on a park bench, I opened my sack and ate the *Baby Ruth* bar in it. As the sun set I began to feel alone and a little scared. A couple of strange looking people walked by me, staring. Running away from their creepy grins, I bumped into a policeman.

"Whoa, fella, what's your hurry?" The burly looking cop gave me a friendly smile as he asked the question.

I began to stutter about needing to get home in a hurry.

"And where is home? You're not lost, are you?" He seemed to have a sense that I wasn't being honest with him—or that I was indeed lost.

Panicking, I ignored Jim's advice about steering clear of a policeman and blurted out, "I need to find my brother, Bob Kropp. He's in the army here in Baltimore.

The next thing I knew, I was sitting in a police station and phone calls were made until they located Bob. Unfortunately, there was nothing he could do with me. He was in basic training. His life was no longer his own. He belonged to Uncle Sam and could not take in his little runaway brother.

He talked to me on the phone, but he wasn't allowed to leave camp to come and see me. "Aw, Billy, how'd you get out here? I wish I could come and get you, but I can't. I'm in the Army. I'll be heading overseas pretty soon. They won't let me leave base. You shouldn't have come out here. They'll have to call Mom and Dad; there's nothing else to do."

I felt betrayed. Calling Mom and Dad was the worse fate. I could only imagine what my punishment would be when I got home to them. They couldn't come for me right away, however, so I was sent to a juvenile detention facility. It was another boys' home in the Baltimore area.

I'll never forget that experience either. There was a fellow there they called "Mr. Bounce." He would grab you by the hair of your head and bounce you off the tile in the bathroom. When I was caught smoking, he made me chew a bag of tobacco and swallow it. I'm sure I've felt pretty sick at different times in my life, but I recall that as the sickest I've ever been. Turning every shade of green imaginable, I gagged as he stood over me, forcing me to chew and swallow every bit of that pouch of tobacco. When I vomited, he made me clean it up. It should have turned me off from the stuff, but only long enough until I got out of that torture chamber called a boys' home.

That's the kind of place it was. Mr. Bounce had a 2X4 that he had wrapped with a gunnysack on one end so it wouldn't leave marks. It was a different time. Places like that got by with that sort of thing. I'm not saying I didn't deserve some type of punishment, but the treatment I got made me think it was my lot in life, that I deserved nothing better. Why wouldn't I feel that way—I was just passed from one place of horror to another.

I don't remember the name of that place and it is probably for the best that I don't. The Kropps came and got me and took me home. Although relieved to be out from under the "care" of Mr. Bounce, I wasn't looking forward to going back to my previous existence.

All throughout the journey home, I was berated and reminded that I would never amount to anything, that I was the worthless illegitimate son of a roadhouse prostitute, the "Bad Seed." That's who I would always be.

"I don't know what we could have been thinking taking you in and trying to raise you as our own son. We've given you every advantage to live a good, clean life. Just look at your brother, Bob, how handsome and respectable he looks in his uniform."

Carrying on until I just shut her words out of my mind, I closed myself into my own world that did not include Mrs. Kropp.

Chapter Four
Not A Typical Teen

When I reached fourteen, I should have been enjoying life, thinking about girls and cars. Instead all I could seem to do was get into trouble. I was growing into the physique of a young man. That did not seem to alter Mrs. Kropp's view of me. I was nothing but trouble to her and she was determined to take me down, domineer me into subjection, and abuse was the means she used.

For some reason I did not use my size or strength against her. She had beaten me down enough that I accepted my lot in life and our relationship. She was a domineering parent figure that seemed to think the only way to control me was through torture and abuse. In our travesty of a "family," the household was what she dictated it would be. Bob was now absent from this bizarre horror of a home environment. The Korean conflict was in full gear and he was sent there. While that was a distraction for a time, this half-demented tyrannical shrew eventually took all her pent up angst and worry over him out on me.

Suzie was the light of all our lives. She had outlived the doctor's prognosis at this time by four years. At age nine, she was still the sweetest little thing. She was very small for her age, but did not lack at all in intelligence. She could not always attend school because of her physical limitations, but absorbed knowledge at an amazing pace. She was an avid reader and would sit and tell me stories she read with such excitement, I felt I had read them myself.

I was still illiterate and reminded continually of how stupid I was because I couldn't read. I'd never had any incentive to improve myself. My foremost goal in life was to get to be old enough to leave the Kropp house, get a job, and be on my own. The problem was that I got in trouble so often, it was becoming more and more apparent I would not make it beyond prison. That was drummed into my head until I came to the conclusion that prison would be much better than living under the same roof with Mrs. Kropp.

She still would tie me to the radiator. The difference now was that I was able to figure out ways of getting loose and would run off to get into more trouble.

Many times I was escorted home by the local constable because I'd vandalized a local business or stolen something from the five and ten cent store. It got to the point that I was banned from most stores in town. Most fellows my age had newspaper routes, played sports in school, and their greatest "sins" were sneaking off to smoke occasionally. I'd been smoking since I was nine. I had no desire to get a job because I knew I wouldn't be able to keep any of the money I earned.

The times that Mr. Kropp took me to the Bakery with him, it gave me a reprieve from spending my day under the stern gaze of Mrs. Kropp. She worked hard to find things to accuse me of doing. When nothing presented itself—although I was usually more than willing to oblige her by doing something worthy of punishment—she would come up behind me, twist my ear between her fingers, pinching and twisting until I yelled from the pain. There would be no reason behind the attack, it just seemed to either give her sadistic pleasure to see me suffer or it released some heinous delight to hear me holler.

Suzie's blue eyes glistened with tears when she witnessed Mrs. Kropp's mistreatment of me. Seeing the sympathy on her little face made me feel worse than any suffering I endured. She was the reason I never struck out at my tormentor. I was also aware that Suzie prayed for me. Several times I would pass by her room and hear her crying, calling out my name to God. I'm not sure where she received her faith and teaching about God. It was as if she was an angel, sent on a mission to give a sliver of hope and light to my otherwise dark and dismal existence. It was unreal for me to realize she had the maturity and insight to pray for her miserable wretch of a brother. Her heart of compassion was amazing.

Her birth defect hindered her from venturing very far from home. So there she remained most days, never wavering in her love for me nor veering from giving joy to everyone around her.

Mrs. Kropp kept me from enjoying my little sisters' company much. As always, I was made to feel an outsider to the family unit. If I showed attention or affection to my siblings, I would be scolded and told to stay away from baby Joanne or to stop pestering Suzie.

"You are a horrid nuisance and a black sheep of this family. I don't know what I've ever done to deserve such a miserable, disobedient, and troublesome child." Mrs. Kropp would shake her head in dismay as she frequently reminded me of who I was and who I was not.

I got so I avoided being at home. But when I wasn't home, it was difficult for me to escape the local law. Local wooded areas were my favorite hiding places when the weather was mild. After stealing food from grocery stores for some time, I quickly upgraded to stealing liquor from liquor stores. Drinking was my favorite past time. I did manage to hang with a few friends of like passions. We'd get into trouble together, be banned from seeing each other, and just go from one escapade to another. We were on a fast track to a life of crime.

When I turned sixteen, there was no longer any need for a pretense of my attending school. Still unable to read or write, I was at least free of putting forth the effort to go and sit in a classroom and pretend to do so.

I needed to get out on my own, get away from my "family." The plan was to rob the general store. Hiding behind one of the counters toward the back of the store, I intended to help myself to whatever I wanted after the proprietor locked up for the night. I hadn't drafted a complete plan of how I would escape after getting a good "haul."

When the lights were turned out and the door was locked, I emerged from my hiding place. Grabbing some candy, I stuffed my mouth with chocolate and roamed around stuffing things in my pockets. Grabbing a bag, I went to the locked cage that served as the town's post office.

Without thinking through what I was doing, I was about to commit a federal crime; prying open the door of the steel cage, I managed to get to the cash drawer. Stuffing the bills into the paper bag in my hand, I felt pretty cool. This was the biggest and best I'd accomplished. I didn't have long to enjoy the thrill I felt at pulling off a real "grown up" robbery.

I was busted as I made my attempt at leaving the store with my loot.

Chapter Five
Prison or the Military

I was scared spitless. The judge peered down at me. His steely gray eyes could have bored a hole right through to the depth of my soul. I felt two inches tall.

"Young man, you are on your way to a life of crime. Right now you are bound for federal prison. I don't know if you realize what that means, but it won't be pretty!"

Continuing, he spewed through loose dentures, "You've committed a federal crime. You broke into the post office. That's a federal offense. Did you know that? Stealing money from Uncle Sam is not a very smart thing to do."

He paused, letting his words penetrate my thoughts. Thrusting a paper in front of my face, he snarled, "You have a few hours to read this and decide: the federal penitentiary for 20 years or join the army. Either way you may get some sense knocked into that head of yours."

I stared at the paper. I couldn't read or write. Any time I'd spent in a classroom had been torture for me. I was bullied, picked fights, got suspended, skipped school, did everything but learn. Ashamed that I could not read, I pretended to take in the words written on the paper. Even without reading it, I understood the judge's edict: prison or the army. My brother, Bob, was in Korea. That would be my option.

The judge stood, gathered his flowing robe around him, and stated more than asked, "You are seventeen, aren't you? You have to be seventeen to get into the army. If that's what you decide to do, report back here in two hours with your birth certificate. The deputy will escort you to the recruiting office."

Trying to hide my panic, I nodded agreement. I turned to go but the judge summoned me back.

"This is what happens when you commit a federal crime, William! That little cage you broke into at the store is considered the property of the federal government. It's a post office. When you stole from that register, you were stealing from Uncle Sam—now we'll give him a chance to get his money back!"

His chuckle grated on my nerves. I didn't see any humor in his remark. My mind was churning. I wondered how far I could get if I ran. He wouldn't be looking for my return for two hours. I could steal a car, but I would probably get farther walking—the car would be too easy to track.

Heading down the courthouse steps, I saw Mrs. Kropp at the bottom. How was I going to run now? She reached out, jerked my shoulder, and began reminding me again how worthless I was all the way back to the house.

Despite the fact I could fight and beat someone twice my size, she still held me in the grip of fear. Although I hated her with a passion, I cowered under her gaze and derision.

Stammering I said, "I need my birth certificate. The judge wants me to come back and go into the army."

"Well, that will be good riddance and hopefully they'll get something through that thick head of yours."

As she spoke she went to a drawer and pulled the document out, handing it to me.

"There, go to your room, comb your hair and wash your face. I won't have my son disgracing the family, looking like you never wash."

Taking the certificate from her hand, I hatched a plan. There was a pen on my dresser. I knew how to write numbers so as neatly as I could, I changed the 5 to a 4, so it would appear that I was born in 1934, making me seventeen.

Apprehension overwhelmed me as I returned to the courthouse. I was afraid the clerk would notice my feeble attempt at changing the date of my birth. I also began to feel a bit of excitement at the prospect of joining the army. I knew we were at war with North Korea, but that didn't concern me. To this point my life had been a hell on earth—it couldn't get any worse, or so I thought.

Neither the judge nor his clerk made any comment about my date of birth. Either they noticed my attempt at making myself appear 17 and didn't care, or did not look at it carefully. I was basic training bound at the age of 16.

I was sent to Ft. Riley, Kansas. The temperature there during that training was 101 degrees. For some reason my drill sergeant hated me. I'm sure I must have been an obnoxious idiot. Maybe I just had it written on my face: *Hate me, I'm a worthless, good-for-nothing piece of humanity.*

Whatever the reason, he hated me. Often he would come up behind me and shout, "Down on your face, Kropp, give me 25."

There were four platoons in training. The sergeants put together a competition. I won the contest by doing 114 pushups. The sarge slapped me on the back and said, "Glad to see you're growing up to be a man, son."

In retrospect, I wonder if rather than hating me, he was doing me a favor, getting me in shape—not just for the inter platoon competition, but for what was ahead of me. Perhaps he was conditioning me.

From there I was shipped to Korea where it was 30 below zero. The drastic temperature shock to my system was debilitating at first. I was in a different world in more ways than the temperature. We were in the mountains. I clearly remember the name as *Pork Chop Ridge*.

Before entering the service, I had acquired a couple of habits. Smoking and chewing tobacco was something I'd done for years. Alcohol had also become a part of my life and often got me into trouble. It had begun to dominate my life.

While I drank some beforehand, now in the army I immersed myself in drinking. I'm not sure where we got them, but there was an abundant supply of small bottles of whiskey, the kind you got on airplanes. There were bushel baskets full of them with no end to the supply.

I was in a drunken stupor all the time. Taking my three canteens, I filled them with alcohol from those little bottles and drank non-stop. Having lived a life of loneliness and unhappiness, I was a prime contender for the army life in the middle of a war. Talk about conditioning to face hardship, I'd been conditioned to face death without much concern about whether I lived or died.

My seventeenth birthday was celebrated in a foxhole on June 1, 1952 there in Korea. I was now old enough to be in the army, even though I'd already been there about nine months.

The army experience, thrust into the middle of the Korean War, was a shock. Even though my life prior to that time was anything but pleasant, this was nothing that could really have prepared me to face that war. It was not at all what I'd expected. There were many days when I considered the judge's other option—locked up behind bars— would have been better.

While much of my time in Korea is stored back in the recesses of my mind never to be opened up, there were a few things that stick out as especially horrifying. One day we were sent out on patrol and had been away from camp for days. Walking through a rice paddy, I stepped on the body of a Korean soldier. My foot sank above my ankle into his rotting belly. To this day, I can't put my feet into mud without getting nauseous. Of all the days where I saw death and the gruesome reality of war, that one event stands out in my mind.

There was a fifty-caliber machine gun nest on each side of a platoon. It is a large gun and took three to operate it: one to feed the ammo, one to keep things coordinated, and the last to fire the gun—I was the gunner.

Shorty Mills was the guy who fed my gun. We became friends quickly. He was just the kind of guy you couldn't help but like. He was not very tall—obviously where he got his nickname—and he just had a way about him. We had an immediate connection, although there was something about him that really got on my last nerve. He carried a little New Testament in his pocket, which he read when there was a lull. The worse thing he did was quote Scripture to me. The one he quoted the most, the one that really got me angry was: *For God so loved the world that He gave His only begotten Son, that Whosoever believes in Him will not perish, but have everlasting life.* John 3:16.

He would look at me and say, "You know, Bill, you can put your name right in there: 'For

God so loved Bill Kropp that He gave His only begotten Son, that if Bill Kropp believes in Him, he will not perish, but have everlasting life."

Then he'd flash a huge grin at me, slap me on the back and tell me how much God loved me. I didn't have the strength to argue with him, but I would throw down a few swigs from my canteen and curse him and his Scripture. Nothing seemed to faze Shorty.

I knew he had a wife and two kids. He talked about them and how much he missed them. He carried their pictures inside his New Testament. I could tell he was the kind of dad I always wished I had had.

His prayers were more aggravating. During times when we weren't firing the gun and late at night even though he was quiet, I knew when he was praying. I don't know how I knew, I just did. It really bothered me. But I liked Shorty.

We were situated in such a way that we could observe the North Koreans at different times when we were not in battle mode. We could see them playing volleyball. I was itching to fire my gun—not at them, of course, without being commanded to do so—but at the volleyball. I figured I could hit it and scare them pretty well. I wanted to do that so bad.

My commander nixed that idea pretty fast when he got wind of it. As drunk as I was all the time, it's a wonder I didn't go ahead with my idea.

I'd never been big on obeying orders—just ask my adoptive mother. I managed to hold off on that urge, however. It would not have been a good outcome had I played out my imagination.

The battle got pretty fierce on Pork Chop Ridge one day and we were taking a lot of losses. It didn't look good, but we kept at our post.

I believe it was a hand grenade that hit our nest. It blew us in different directions. I was pretty well soused on my little liquor bottles. Maybe that's why I wasn't killed. I was blown out and away from the gun. Stumbling around, I found Shorty. He was blown to pieces. My only real buddy in my whole life. I was outraged at God. Standing over him in my drunken stupor, I said to him, "Where's your 'whosoever believes will have everlasting life' now, Shorty? You're gone, and I'm here. Why not me? You've got a wife and two kids waiting for you to come home."

I don't know how long I stood there weeping in anguish over the broken body of my friend, but at some point, our camp was overrun and we were captured—those of us that were alive. We were hog-tied with our hands behind our backs and loaded into dump trucks. Thrown in like garbage, we were pretty banged up and bruised and more so on the ride over rough terrain.

It seemed like we rode forever. They took us to a POW camp where holes were dug into the ground. These holes were 15 or 16 feet long and 4 or 5 feet wide. We were put into insulated outfits and thrown into the hole. Sixteen men shared the hole I was put into. The pit was then covered with a steel frame with barbed wire across the entire top.

How we survived on the meager portions of food we were allotted is a miracle. Rice was thrown to us once a day. There were a couple of tin cups we shared as we attempted to eat and drink the water they allowed us. There was no sanitation. The water was foul and the rice rancid.

We lived like animals. We were not taken out to use the bathroom. Everything we did was done there in that gross hole in the ground. It's difficult to give an accurate description of the hellhole we occupied. If anyone attempted to raise their head to peer through the wire covering the pit, a North Korean soldier would take the butt end of his rifle and whack him in the head.

There were several of these pits dug into the flat surface of ground all over this POW camp. I'm not sure of the exact number, but there were several. Each one, of course, held around the same number of men as ours—16 or so. There were two buildings in this compound. One housed the Korean military; the other was used to prepare their meals and our sparse offerings.

There were three guys in our hole that used to quote Scripture every day. I was beside myself with frustration. Why did I have to get thrown in with these religious nuts? First there had been Shorty Mills—I put up with him because I liked him—but I felt like killing these three. They prayed for every one of us by name every single day and night.

If I could have had the room to get a hold of their throats, I would have strangled the life from them, silencing their voices. Trying to jump from one end of the hole to the other through the filthy, bony bodies of my fellow soldiers, I tried to stop them, but nothing seemed to deter them—not my vile curses against them or my weak attempts to throttle them.

Six months passed as we counted the days, struggling to maintain our sanity. It was 1953 and I was almost 19 years old.

From the bowels of the pits around us, we could hear the anguished cries of the men that would lose their minds, unable to cope with the awful conditions. The guards would crush their skulls, beating them back as they forced their heads up, shredding their faces on the barbed wire. Out of their minds, they would thrash back and forth against the wire, slicing their faces until the blood poured copiously.

The day came when we heard planes overhead. The obvious confusion around us told it was American planes. Our military were not aware that this was a POW camp—their intelligence showed it to be some type of ammunition installation. The flat ground with the pits dug were not identified by air as the prison it was.

The bombs started dropping. That's when the North Koreans went berserk. They opened the pits, herding us at gunpoint back to the dump trucks. In the confusion of bombs piercing the night air, exploding all around us, three of us escaped into the woods. There may have been others who did the same—if so, we did not see them. The three of us took off at a dead run, determined to be free. Our feeling was that if we were shot, it would be much better than the existence we had suffered for the past six months.

Chapter Six
Our Goal: The 38th Parallel

Running without looking back, I kept going, my chest hurting, pushing, pushing until my legs gave out and I collapsed. My two POW companions were just steps behind me. Tony tripped over me and sprawled on the damp underbrush.

Ralph saw we'd stopped and joined us on the forest floor. We were all exhausted and out of breath. Ralph said what we all knew, "Fellas, we've got to keep moving. They may not know we're gone yet, but if they discover us missing, the woods will be filled with them. Come on, get up."

I couldn't imagine how I was going to get back up. Every part of me hurt. Taking a breath was painful, every nerve and muscle seemed wracked with pain. For six months we'd been cramped in a space where we couldn't stand up without space to move about. Every muscle in my body had atrophied. How we'd managed to sprint away and escape was beyond reason. It had been a reflex reaction, moving our legs robotically. It had to have been sheer adrenaline that drove us as far as we'd come.

Knowing Ralph spoke the truth, I touched Tony's arm. "He's right, we've got to keep going." I gasped out the words.

Gathering all the strength I could, I tried to pull myself to my feet. I'd been fed a starvation portion of rice and water for 6 months. When I had arrived in Korea, I weighed about 180 lbs. I was now down to about 120, and had not only been deprived of exercise, but also was covered in sores from all the filth and squalor I'd been living in. The three of us were not in any condition to trek through the woods and out of the mountains. For someone physically fit from weeks of training, it would have been difficult. Our trio, skin stretched over weak bones was in no shape for the task, fueled solely by the remote prospect of staying out of the hellhole we'd escaped.

Knowing my survival depended on it, I pushed myself forward. However, while I'd been running before, I now was able to only drag myself a step at a time. As we struggled to keep moving, we listened for any indication that we were being pursued. Evidently our captors were too occupied with the bombing and transporting the other POW's to miss us or to pursue us.

We were in a massive forest covering a mountain. We knew we had to move down off the mountain and head south with hopes of reaching the 38th parallel where we would be out of the danger of recapture by the North Koreans. Our situation was pretty hopeless. In enemy territory, surrounded by towns and villages filled with Communist sympathizers, we didn't stand a chance.

Without food, without strength, dressed as prisoners, we were sitting ducks, ready to be picked off by the first person to come across us.

Stopping to rest beside a bubbling brook, we gulped down the crystal clear water. I'm sure we were in a state of dehydration from the previous months without good water, having suffered frequent bouts of dysentery. Our flight for freedom drained what little moisture we had. Still in our insulated garments, we decided to keep them for the times we would stop and sleep, but otherwise shed them when we went in search of food.

Unable to continue, we took a chance and rested for several hours, knowing there was no way we could go on without it. When we woke, it was dark with only a shaft of subdued moonlight filtering through the dense trees. We agreed it would be safest to move under the cover of night.

Our rumbling stomachs ached. The food provision in the POW camp had left us hungry all the time. This was a new and powerful pain. We were starving to death.

To say we were in a state of panic is an understatement. Energy for our journey was vital. No matter how desperate our commitment to survival, without food, we could not go on. Before heading out, we again took advantage of the clear stream, not knowing when we'd find water again. There was nothing to put the water into.

The plan was to follow the stream as long as possible, continuing to move southward toward our goal. We forced ourselves to eat some grass and green foliage from the forest floor. The taste was awful. Ralph insisted anything green would give us energy.

"It's the chlorophyll," he insisted. "I learned about it in science class."

I thought Ralph was just being a smart aleck, but I didn't care; I'd do what I had to do to survive. Why I wanted to live at that point, I'm not sure. Probably because I'd survived so much I was determined to do everything I could to keep alive. I ate the stupid grass, angry at Ralph all the time I ingested it. He couldn't seem to shut up about something called *photosynthesis* and how it was connected to green things that grow. If I'd had the strength, I would have shut him up. It didn't take long, however, for me to realize how desperately the three of us needed each other.

Foraging for food continued to be our greatest challenge as we made our way down the mountain. Villages were scarce. At night we pilfered through garbage when we came upon a small village. Rotten fish, discarded roots of vegetables, and many unidentifiable things were eaten. The rankest odors made it impossible to keep from vomiting at times. This was something we avoided, knowing it would increase dehydration and not offer any ease to the horrible stomach cramps that come with starvation.

I learned to hold my nose and eat fast. It was agonizing to hide close to a village where we could smell food being prepared as we waited for nightfall to travel and forage. Lying low and out of sight was a struggle as our bellies cried painfully for something delectable. Later at night, we'd fight animals for leftover grease thrown out on the ground. Lapping it up, chewing on the grease-saturated grass was a real treat. It was so much better than our usual fare of discarded garbage.

A Korean hut on the mountainside would not, of course, contain refrigeration and shelves stocked from a grocery store. Their meager cupboards held very little and did not allow for waste. Our options for tasty morsels were slim to none.

Pushing forward proved more difficult with the passing of each day. I'd been hungry many times during my short life but never knew the pain of real hunger. Doubled over, unable to stand, we often crawled ahead, knowing it was vital we keep moving, always under the cover of night.

Ralph must have had some training as a scout. He helped us be inventive with what we found along the way. Soon we learned to be careful even with the garbage we found but more often than not, we were so anxious to ease the hunger pangs, we inhaled the most unseemly things.

We began to take turns foraging for food after nightfall. It turned into a competition for Ralph and me. We tried to be creative in bringing back a "meal" we could share. Tony was too weak to try to find food on his own. It took all his strength to keep up with us when we moved forward. He was a hindrance, slowing us down, but never once did we consider leaving him behind.

Although our hunger was never satisfied, it was a real treat when one of us emerged from our "hunting" expedition with a bowl of goat's milk or some oversized beetles. Believe it or not, the crunch and juice from the bugs became a delicacy to us. They often had a sweet taste that made us wish for more when we'd eaten all that were gathered.

I recall vividly one night when I'd been sent to scout out something to eat. The past few days had produced very little and discouragement was heavy in our little band of three. I was determined not to return to Ralph and Tony until I could deliver something extra special. The overgrowth of forest was thinning which meant there were more small homes with chickens and sometimes a cow or a couple of goats roaming in the yards. Spotting a few scrawny chickens, I figured there would be eggs. I knew Tony, as well as Ralph and I, needed the protein of an egg. I salivated as I crept close to the yard.

Ralph had managed to steal a cup and a bowl a few nights before. I was armed with both, hoping to get some goat's milk and at least three eggs. I knew that grabbing eggs out from under a "sitting" hen would be a challenge, but I was up for it.

The struggle between the hen and me was not only difficult, but also very noisy. She protested with vigor and loud clucking. But nothing was going to stop me. With an egg in each pocket and one in the cup I carried, I fought the temptation to crack one egg and down it immediately—but I resisted.

Following a very thin, roving goat was making me dizzy. I finally succeeded in pinning her against the outer wall of a small dilapidated shed. Filling the small bowl I had with milk was not too difficult; unfortunately a lot of yard dirt was in the bowl as well.

Finally successful, as I turned to find my way back to my two fellow escapees, I came face-to-face with a very small boy. He may have been a lot older than he appeared, but he seemed very small. His eyes were wide with a mixture of fear and anger. They were fixed on my prize, the bowl of tainted milk and the egg in my cup. He couldn't see the two eggs in my pockets.

He didn't cry out to spread an alarm; he just stared hungrily at my "supper." I'm not sure if he lived in the shabby hut that went with the chickens and goat or if he, like me, was scavenging for survival. Despite my extreme hunger, he pulled at my emotions. He reminded me of another boy, another time, banished to the porch, without supper, and I remembered my brother Bob bringing me a half sandwich and a glass of milk. That memory of how hungry I was then and how good that cold milk with the peanut butter sandwich felt sliding down my throat stopped me in my tracks.

My instinct was to take my prize and run. I knew I could outrun the boy who had made no attempt to betray my presence with a shout. Without a second thought though, I handed him the bowl of milk and the egg. I kept the cup—regretting only that I no longer had the bowl. His smile was all I had to sate my empty gullet as I hurried back to Ralph and Tony with an egg for each.

"Where's yours?" Ralph questioned.

"Couldn't wait," I responded and changed the subject. "I was almost discovered, however, and ended up leaving the bowl behind."

Ralph shrugged as he swallowed his egg. Giving a sigh and rubbing his sunken stomach he said, "I'll try to get another tomorrow night. Thanks for dinner, 'Mom'." He laughed.

I'll say this about Ralph, if you're going to have to travel down a mountainside in North Korea, fearing for your life, without proper nourishment or any comfort, he's the travel companion to have. He kept a sense of humor and really did have a lot of survival skills to share with us.

I lay down on the mossy ground that night, with a hollow void in my stomach but satisfaction about the smile on the face of the little North Korean boy that gulped down my egg and the milk for our trio. What the other two fellows didn't know, wouldn't hurt them.

Kimchi was a favorite meal of the Koreans. It consisted of fermented vegetables such as cabbage, radishes, scallions or cucumbers. To me it was nasty when first prepared; when we rarely found leftover garbage of the dish, it was putrid. Drinking the rotting juice of this turned my stomach and I often opted for dirt and grass. Ralph, always the "dietician," would urge me to try to eat the discarded Kimchi for my health.

Raiding a North Korean family's vegetable garden was considered a banquet feast. This happened seldom. They kept their vegetables picked clean and any excess stored inside their hovels. I doubt they suspected escaped POW's would be looking to steal from them. Their own North Korean soldiers had little to eat, as did their neighbors. Watching any growth of a cabbage or cucumber was a family project. Unfortunately this meant very little for Ralph, Tony, and me when we came upon a garden plot.

Tony couldn't have weighed more than 80 pounds when we escaped the camp. We saw him grow weaker with the passing of each day. It took us two weeks to reach the bottom of the mountain. We were glad to see flat land and rice fields, but feared we would be discovered out in the open.

While the forest-lined mountain was difficult, at least we had good shelter from discovery.

Again, we traveled only under the protection of dark. Always heading south, our feelings wavered from thinking we were going to make it to safety, to wanting to just lie down and die in North Korea. That thought ultimately kept us going, though; none of us wanted to have North Korea as our final resting place.

Finding shelter to sleep in during the day was dangerous. A dilapidated shed was usually our choice. One evening when we went to wake Tony so we could head out, he was stone cold. Covering him the best we could, we knew we couldn't linger but had to move on. Our remorse, though brief, was sincere. He'd been our companion for six months in the pit at the POW camp and now for weeks on the run following our escape. It had been "all for one and one for all" as we ran for safety. We didn't have the strength to weep over Tony. He had not been able to fight off the infections that were ravaging our bodies. Ralph and I reverently turned from Tony's body and headed forward; self-preservation was our primary thought and motivation. There was nothing we could do to help our friend.

Ralph was probably the strongest of us, but he faltered many times, falling down and saying, "I can't go on. The pain in my gut is too much. I just can't go on."

Looking back, I suppose we spurred each other on. When one of us was ready to give up, the other would goad the other to continue. I knew one thing: I didn't want Tony's fate, being left to rot in North Korea.

We pushed on each day, still moving south. Villages were now more plentiful. Scavenging food was a bit more successful as well, but the threat of discovery a much higher risk. We didn't dare seek help in any village. It could have been possible that we'd find an American sympathizer that didn't like the communists. But it was a risk not worth taking. There was no way I was going back to a cage in the ground. At least the air we were breathing was not fetid with the stench of human excrement.

As the weeks passed, we grew thinner and weaker. I'm sure we resembled skeletons covered in skin. We were starving, filthy, only moving ahead as robots. We'd set our sights on our goal—the 38th parallel. Numb from fatigue, we mechanically followed our routine: find a place to rest during the day, forage for food and water and travel at night. Sharing every morsel of food, our camaraderie was a major factor in our survival.

Most of my memory of the three months we walked through North Korea is a blur. My brain could only accommodate the thoughts that kept our goal in sight. Nothing else mattered, nothing else was stored in my memory bank. Every organ of my body, every cell, all the processing of thought was dying, starving for what was necessary to keep me alive. What we were able to find and eat was too meager to nourish anything but the survival mode—move and keep moving or die in enemy territory.

There are no amusing anecdotes to offer or even amazing moments of escape from discovery. If there were some of those, they are lost in the myriad of minute-by-minute struggles we endured through exhaustion and starvation, with an innate power of preservation pushing us forward.

Three months into our quest to find an American camp, we found ourselves out in the open at dawn. A man driving a horse-drawn wagon was on top of us before we realized it. Because we could see him, we knew he could see us as well.

Weary and too weak to run and with no visible place to hide, we took a big risk and spoke to him. He was Korean. Since we were in North Korea, we assumed he was North Korean. He understood us well enough to offer us a ride to the 38th parallel where we would hopefully be able to cross from enemy lines to freedom. We were still in grave danger and our presence with him would put him in as much or more danger if caught. As a North Korean aiding the enemy, he would surely be put to death.

Completely at his mercy, we hoped he was planning to help us, not turn us in for a reward for capturing enemy soldiers. Fatigued and weak, we climbed into his wagon.

He had something in the back of his wagon to cover us. Crawling under it, for the first time on our journey we were moving in daylight. Covered as we were, we had no idea what was happening around us. When the wagon slowed, my heart would pound with fear. There was no real reason this lone Korean should help us. But it seems we had stumbled on a fellow that either had more compassion than politics on his mind or he was an Angel sent to rescue us. Personally, I never had a moment's thought about Heavenly help. My most recent feelings about God or religion related to my three antagonists in the POW camp. They'd angered me until I felt like killing them. Shorty Mills' death added God to my "hate list" and I was too busy shaking with fear to even consider that my sister Suzie might be praying for me.

The heat of the sun warmed us under our tarp-like covering. With no meat on our bones we were cold continually. The comfort of our cozy cocoon gave opportunity for a nap. How I managed to sleep under the circumstances, I don't know—it was probably the first time I'd been comfortable and warm. Anyway, I slept as the wagon lumbered over rough road, still in enemy territory.

Before nightfall, the wagon came to a halt. Our benefactor pulled back our cover and gave a toothless grin.

"You here, buddies! You safe now!"

Unable to believe our ears, we didn't move. Staring at our rescuer, the realization that we were "home-free" registered in our dulled senses.

Scrambling to get up, I climbed over the edge of the wagon, amazed to see that we were just outside of an American army camp in South Korea.

Dehydration held the tears at bay that choked me. I couldn't speak. Stumbling toward our wagon driver, I embraced him and shook with tearless sobs. Ralph grabbed my neck and collapsed to the ground. Neither of us had the strength to express what we were feeling inside. In fact, I wondered if it were a dream; how could I be sure this was real?

Both Ralph and I lay in a heap where we landed. I thought I was laughing and crying at the same time but was never sure.

In short order, we were swarmed by U.S. servicemen in awe of our condition. Struggling to speak, it was Ralph who finally spit out that we were POW's, escaped from a North Korean camp.

It had taken us a full three months to travel from the POW camp to the 38th parallel. The little Korean who rescued us and took us the last leg of our journey did not linger after delivering us to our destination. I cannot remember having a conversation with him at any time after we were taken into the camp.

At that time, although I was happy to be free, thoughts of the miraculous still escaped me. I maintained that I'd journeyed from the POW camp to the 38th parallel on my own power and by my own strength. I recognized the help of my companions Tony and Ralph, but that was the extent of my thoughts.

Weighing in at 80 pounds, I was sent to Japan to recuperate. It was a slow process before I could eat regular food and begin to gain strength. I was kept at the hospital in Japan for two months before being sent back to the states.

Happy to be alive and able to eat and drink when and what I pleased, I didn't share Ralph's excitement about going home. I never considered that I had a home and the lonely feelings of rejection and anger settled back in on me. Going "home" was just an expression to me with no anticipation or joy. I would have been delighted to stay in Japan. I enjoyed being pampered by the hospital staff. It was such a relief to sleep on a comfortable bed.

Chapter Seven
Post War

Picking up my drinking habit where I left off was not hard. Alcohol was plentiful and I was eager to drown my experiences in a sea of inebriation. Thrilled when I received my back pay of over four thousand dollars after I landed in Seattle, Washington, my first state-side destination after being released from the hospital was to hit the bars and celebrate my freedom from despair and captivity.

I don't have a clue what I did while in Seattle. Most of my money was gone when I woke up on a train, headed to an army base in Mineral Wells, Texas. I was hung over and eager to get my next drink. The sound of the train pounded through my head like a sledgehammer.

I don't know what I expected out of the town that housed the army base—all I cared about was whether or not there was a tavern. I planned that to be my first stop after checking in with my gear.

Mineral Wells was a town of about 300 people and a troop population of around 7,000. The sidewalks were rolled up around 6 p.m. each evening. It was known that the war would soon be over. A treaty had been signed; the war was winding down and would soon come to a close. I was still in the army and technically, we were still at war so all rules regarding conduct during wartime were in full force.

My status had been elevated. Promotions came on a rotation basis and I was now a Master Sergeant. So many had either died in the war or been discharged because of injuries, my upgrade was automatic. There was nothing I did personally that merited the advancement in rank.

My drinking escalated. I would drink and drink, and drink some more. My regular consumption was 3 or 4 fifths of whiskey each day. With my alcohol consumption came fighting and just getting in trouble on a daily basis—it took me only six months to be demoted to a Private. My downward spiral was in high gear. It appeared that my experiences in Korea had done nothing to teach me responsibility. I still fitted well the title of "Bad Seed."

While on Honor Guard duty, I was called in to guard because the guard on duty got sick. I was completely wasted. Here I was standing guard, armed with a loaded machine gun, drunk as a skunk. My condition was probably not noted because it was my usual state of awareness, or lack thereof.

The commanding officer's jeep approached my station. I was sure I hollered "Halt" but who knows if I did or not as drunk as I was. The vehicle kept coming. I lowered my gun and emptied it into the front of the CO's jeep. I raised my weapon to fire again, but it was empty of ammunition. I dread to think of the results had my weapon contained any bullets. I could have killed the CO and his driver.

That little stunt got me a court martial. What I'd done could carry a life sentence—firing on an officer. In wartime it could even carry a death sentence. Here I was, a survivor of a Korean POW Camp with a miraculous escape from enemy territory, then after a two-month hospital stay, I was brought back to life, only to get myself in a real pickle after returning stateside.

Unbelievably, I was sentenced to a mere year in the federal penitentiary at Leavenworth, Kansas. The only explanation for the light sentence was my POW status. Of course, I was handed a dishonorable discharge—a disgrace to my uniform—again a reject. I not only felt worthless, I was worthless!

Believe it or not, I was released from Leavenworth after 9 months and 13 days for good behavior—yeah, hard to believe!

Before I could be released, I had to have some place to go—a relative, or someone to come forward and offer me a home. The Red Cross located my biological mother. We had had no contact or relationship for years. She and her third husband came to Leavenworth and picked me up. They took me to their home in Beloit, Wisconsin. I lived with them for not quite a year. I was closing in on twenty-years-old. This is when I discovered I had a biological half-brother, Richard.

Judy was living there in Beloit with my mother. She kept talking to me about her best friend, Deanna. They'd become close during high school and continued to spend a lot of time together. It was Judy's bright idea to set me up with this friend of hers.

I wasn't too excited about the idea. It wasn't that I wouldn't be happy for some female companionship. I was very agreeable to that—I just didn't want some homespun, innocent girl that was a friend of my sister. Who knew what she'd look like?

They both appeared in the doorway one afternoon while I was lazing around the house. The girl, Deanna, looked ridiculous. She was wearing bib overalls that seemed to swallow her. My opinion was that this was one goofy looking girl with her hair in pigtails. I guess she was the epitome of a farm girl, but to me she was just plain ugly. I was devoid of manners, but at least I didn't appraise her lack of appeal in front of the girl. I told Judy my opinion after Deanna left.

"If she's the girl you want to fix me up with, forget it! There's nothing attractive about her."

Judy left the topic alone for a few days and then approached me.

"Bill, I found a beautiful girl and set up a blind date for you."

"No, thanks!" I spewed out a quick response. "I've seen your idea of a good date for me, so I'll find my own girls, thank you."

After much coaxing, I finally agreed to the blind date, thinking I could always ditch the girl and head to the bar for a night of drinking.

Well, when this girl came to the door—Wow! What a doll! She wore a flowing dress that hugged her in just the right places; I was smitten. Her hair hung around her shoulders in soft curls, framing her beautiful face. I couldn't believe it when she told me she was Deanna. I don't know what happened to her between our first encounter and then, but she won my heart that moment, and we began to date. I don't know what my sister Judy was thinking to introduce her sweet friend to such a miserable lump of humanity as me!

Poor Deanna didn't know what she was getting herself into. I was wild, and she was innocent and naïve. I drove a yellow convertible—I've always thought that appealed to her more than I did. We became inseparable. She offered a distraction from my constant drinking, but only when I was around her. Otherwise I was working every angle I could to get extra cash. Most of it was spent on booze and my vehicle.

Our courting was quick—we went together for about five months. I asked her to marry me, but didn't give her a ring. I'd had a few run-ins with the law and while I was madly in love with

Deanna, I hadn't changed one thing regarding my habits or my character.

It was shortly after our "ringless" engagement that I became strongly aware I needed to get out of town. The law was after me. I knew it was just a matter of time before I'd be arrested. Trouble was still my constant companion. Out of necessity, I traveled to Loveland, Colorado where the Kropps were living. The reunion was awkward. Seeing Suzie and Joanne was the only part that warmed my heart. They were genuinely delighted to see me. My little sisters were the only ones who gave me a true feeling of a family connection. Bob was not living at home. He came by to see me, though, and we had a nice visit. Our experiences in Korea gave us things to share that no one else could understand. In a sense, I felt I'd returned "home" because of my siblings.

Things were strained between Mrs. Kropp and me. I was now a man, a man that had experienced the horrors of war and imprisonment. No longer having the power to bully me, she was at a loss at how to respond to my presence. When around each other, we settled upon a distant and quiet relationship.

To say I actively hated her as in the past was not the case. But the wounds of the abuse were both physical and deeply emotional. My thick head of hair hid the scarred places on my skull where her broomstick had split my head open on several occasions. The lingering mental anguish of my childhood with the Kropps still held me imprisoned. I'd escaped the North Korean prison camp and had been released from the Federal Penitentiary, but the walls of my prison of memory held me bound in a way that my other incarcerations never did.

Being in Colorado did not bring any changes to my life. It didn't take long for me to find trouble. It usually followed me and if not, I searched and found it.

I managed to get a job in Loveland and sent Deanna her engagement ring via the U.S. Mail. She was the one shining spot in my existence. The goal of earning the money to get her a ring gave me some purpose. However, keeping a job and putting down roots didn't happen. I was in trouble with the law again and it was time to move on. Drawn by my attraction for Deanna, I headed back to Beloit. I hoped the Sheriff had other petty crimes to worry about besides the numerous thefts I'd been involved in.

Deanna and I set a date to be married—March 10, 1955. Now twenty, it was time for me to settle down. Deep down, I believe I hoped that marriage would be the answer to my happiness. I was in love and knew Deanna loved me. After all, if she didn't, she'd have walked away from me as I was no prize.

The day before our wedding, my biological mother and her husband had me arrested for stealing a toolbox from them. They had given me that box. It was the only time I was arrested for something I didn't do. For once I was innocent! What a turn of events. Here they were supposed to be helping me to get acclimated back into society following the war. I have no recollection of what motivated them to accuse me of stealing something they'd given me.

Deanna's mother scraped up the bail of $250 and got me out of jail. We got married in a regular nice church wedding. Deanna was beautiful in her flowing white gown. No doubt the flowers were lovely but I was focused on my bride, still angry with my mother and her husband, and thirsty for a drink other than the punch at the reception, which did not offer alcoholic beverages. I figured Deanna's mother had put all the time, money, and planning into that occasion, she wasn't going to let me ruin the day with my shenanigans.

My life was still on a downhill slide, heading for destruction. The difference was I now had a wife, dragging her along for the dangerous ride.

Chapter Eight
Married Life

We began our life together there in Beloit. I had no trouble getting jobs; I would work just long enough to get a paycheck, get drunk, get in trouble of some kind, and so the cycle continued.

Things got so "hot" with the law, I dragged Deanna back to Colorado. In 1956 our first child, Rosella, was born. She was a beautiful baby girl. Briefly, but not with much commitment, I made an effort to be a responsible husband and father, but alcohol was my first love and it lured me to depths of degradation I'd rather not think about. To tell all the lurid details of my actions and the miserable life I was making for my little family would serve no purpose. There will always be deep regret in the core of my soul for the things Deanna had to endure because of my behavior and lust for liquor.

I would work, get my paycheck, or go on a spree of stealing with some friends and then disappear for two or three days at a time. All the time I was gone I'd be drinking until I'd find myself so hung over I couldn't walk. With the help of friends, I'd manage to head back home. Why Deanna put up with me, I'll never know. Somehow she had the strength of character to keep the commitment she made with me for better or worse. She was certainly getting the "worse" of this deal. Her prayers and faith in God kept her going, one day at a time.

Our second child, Brian, was born in 1958. With our family growing, I still didn't change. How could I? I knew somehow I was destined for disaster. I was a miserable person. I'd been told enough times how worthless I was and I'd proved it repeatedly.

I was always cooking up a scheme to make money. One night a couple of my gang of friends and I got a brilliant idea. We chose a business we were going to rob. Aware that they had a good sized two-door safe, our plan was to break in, take the whole safe with us, then take it to a secluded spot, crack it open and split the proceeds.

Of course, before putting our plan into action, we stopped at the bar and got so drunk we had to hold each other up. My capacity for consumption of alcohol while still remaining ostensibly coherent was highly developed by this time. So I was the "sober" one. We were idiots—no question about it. The alcohol just expanded our moronic capability to plan and carry through our plans.

Various well-meaning people plagued me about getting a decent job, supporting my growing family and becoming a worthwhile citizen. Embarrassed to tell anyone that I could neither read nor write, I just sloughed off all the advice. I knew that any "real" jobs would require literacy. Besides, I was having too much fun drinking, playing with my felon friends, and getting money. I boasted that I was more like Robin Hood than Al Capone. After all, I only stole from the wealthy and gave to the poor—namely, my family and me.

Well, we set off to break into the local market. We were sure there was a sizeable amount of money in the safe. We just had to get it. With three of us, confidence drove us forward, assured that the job was a cinch. Parking in the back alley, we entered the building with little difficulty and found our way to the office where the safe was kept.

Struggling with considerable obstacles, we scooted the heavy iron safe out the door, and next to our vehicle. Our next hurdle was to get the massive thing inside our trunk. Huffing and puffing, straining and lifting, we were able to drop it in the trunk with a bang. I was afraid it had fallen through the floor of the trunk. It hadn't, but the rear end of the old Pontiac came close to hitting the pavement.

Lacking any common sense, we slammed the trunk shut, got into the car, and headed out of the alley and onto the main road. What a sight we must have been when the Sheriff spotted us, headlights beaming almost straight up as the back of the vehicle dragged close to the road.

Familiar with my vehicle, the wise officer pulled behind us and turned on his flashing lights. We knew we'd been had. Stopping beside a cornfield, leaping from the car, we took off, hidden from view by the tall stalks. The excitement of the chase over-powered my state of inebriation and I got away—but I no longer had a car.

But now, the Sheriff was hot on my trail. And he caught up with me. When I was arrested—there at the house, in front of Deanna and my two small children—I should have felt remorse, shame, something. I was just angry.

The Sheriff said I was wanted in regard to thirty-seven armed robberies and this time I wasn't going to get off scot-free. Everything he said just heated my anger higher and higher. By the time we got to the interrogation room, I was at the boiling point.

Being shoved into a chair, I looked around at the officers surrounding me. There were five of them. They began to accuse and question, firing accusations and making demands that I confess.

A big burly officer lunged toward me. Flashes of Mr. Bounce at the juvenile home in Baltimore took focus in my mind. Beside him, a uniformed officer stepped to my side. As he raised his billy club, the image in my brain switched to Mrs. Kropp beating me over the head until she split my head open and the blood ran into my ears and down my neck. From behind me—I think it was the Sheriff—a hand grasped my neck and pushed me forward. Surging through me was the recollection of the time Mother Kropp had beaten me and held my bleeding head over the toilet with her hand firm on the back of my neck.

I don't recall that any of those five officers in that room actually did anything to hurt me. They were, no doubt, trying to intimidate me. But I snapped. My recollections from the abuse of my childhood and the trauma of the POW camp collided and I roared as I stood. Fighting, kicking, punching, charging, I took on all five of the men present. They were left pretty battered and humiliated by the time I was subdued.

Following a brief trial, I was sentenced to ten years in prison, but sent directly to a mental hospital for the criminally insane. My outburst and subsequent attack on the officers is what landed me in the mental ward under lock and key.

My lifestyle had finally caught up with me. I knew that Deanna was expecting our third child; she would be alone for the next ten years. Her parents were very good and would help her as much as they could, but I had to come to grips with the fact I was a miserable failure. I couldn't count one good thing I'd done in my life with the exception of marrying Deanna and fathering two wonderful children. Brian was two and Rosella was four. My only consolation was that they were too young to realize what a worthless bum their father was.

Nothing softened my heart though. I was still the hard-nosed kid, Bill Kropp, son of a roadhouse prostitute, adopted, but unwanted and unloved.

Life was cruel, there was no way around it. If there was a God, He was cruel as well. I still carried hatred for him for Shorty Mills' death, the guy who quoted his Bible religiously every day. What good had it done him?

The hatred I held close for Mrs. Kropp had taken residence with a bitterness that was eating me up. Once when I spent some time in their home after the war, she went to raise her hand at me. I caught her arm and spewed out some of the poisonous venom I carried for her. She backed off—as most bullies do when confronted—and never raised her hand against me again. However, the release of the pent up hatred I threw at her gave me no peace. Like a rattlesnake, releasing venom only gave space to make more. It gnawed at me night and day.

During the years of my marriage to Deanna, I would wake at night screaming in terror, flailing my arms and legs with scenes and experiences from the war as fresh and real there in my dreams as they had been at the time they occurred; the horror of war was still a big part of me. There was no talk at that time of Post-Traumatic Stress Disorder. The war was over but not for the soldiers sent home with as many unseen scars as visible wounds. Missing arms, legs, and head wounds leaving diminished mental capacity were the obvious injuries that needed treatment. Mental anguish left many men crippled emotionally, unable to function normally as beforehand. Battlefront induced alcoholism was commonplace, with little thought or official attention paid to its underlying cause.

The anguish and pain of my tortured life pressed down on me—I was being crushed. Alcohol was my only antidote, my solace but when I came to, with a hang over, the bottomless abysmal pit of war wounds and earlier childhood abuse gaped wider still, oozing hopelessness and sorrow that was more than I could bear.

Now I was sentenced to ten years in prison with my first stint to be served in a mental ward for the criminally insane. I felt like I was going back to the pit in North Korea, only this time all who were held captive with me were already out of their minds.

Chapter Nine
Deanna's story: My Encounter

The judge's words echoed in my mind. "Ten years."

Life with Bill was unstable at best. His drinking binges and absences, doing God only knew what and with whom, left me spending most of my days and nights weeping and praying. I loved Bill and knew he'd been through hell on earth during the war. No matter what, I was always quick to defend him and his actions to others because of that and because of other events in his life.

But, this was a blow—more than I could take. Ten years with two children to raise by myself and another one now growing inside me. My parents were so good to the kids and me. They even showed exceptional patience with Bill.

Dear God, what can I do? You seem so far away. I've prayed and prayed. Bill doesn't change, and I can't raise these children on my own. I just don't have the strength, the energy, or the finances I need for this. I'm out of options, and I guess not even You can do anything with someone so lost as Bill.

I left the courthouse in a fog. There'd been no time to speak to Bill; he was led away in chains. Evidently his behavior at the time of his arrest caused the officials to label him extremely dangerous. The leg chains and handcuffs were deemed necessary for everyone's protection. Even if we could have talked, what could be said? There was no way he could offer help or support for us from the mental ward. While under evaluation by the psychiatrists, I would not even be able to visit him. I had never felt so alone. Even Bill's earlier frequent absences didn't leave me with that feeling because I always knew no matter what, he would eventually find his way home. But now he was out of the picture.

Mechanically I picked the children up from my mother and drove the short distance to our apartment. It was small and nothing special, but I'd always considered it home, sewing curtains to brighten the kitchen and decorating with little inexpensive touches. Today there was no feeling of home. That had been shattered by the judge's sentence, tearing my husband from our lives.

Looking at little Rosella, four-years-old, and Brian, not quite two, my eyes filled with tears. They were so precious and they deserved more than I would ever be able to give them. They deserved a stable home without the hovering shadow of a drunken felon for a father. I didn't want them growing up having to visit him in a mental ward or prison. I knew for certain that would be the sum of their experiences with their father. I would have to do something and right away.

"Finish your supper, kids, we're going to go back to Grandma's house for a few days. Does that sound like fun?"

My voice cracked as I struggled to maintain my composure. Waiting while they finished the meager supper I'd prepared for them, I mulled over in my mind what I must do. Giving them the last of the bread with some peanut butter spread thin to make it go for both, I'd forgone eating so there'd be more for them. Besides, eating was far from my thoughts. My plan did not include eating anything.

"Can I have 'nother sanich, Mama?" Brian's bright blue eyes sparkled as he turned toward me. I turned away, my heart breaking at the sight of this beautiful child I must leave behind. But my resolve was set. I had to do what was best for my children.

"I'm sorry, sweetie. That's all I have. I bet Grandma will have some cookies or cake when we get there." The excitement in Brian's eyes reassured me I was doing the right thing by taking the children to my parents. Thoughts were churning in my mind for an excuse for returning so soon with the kids and not staying there with them. Mother was not aware I was pregnant again.

Earlier as I rifled through my purse while sitting in my dilapidated car outside the courtroom, I confirmed what I already knew. I had one dollar and a few pennies. There was no money to buy food or pay the rent that was overdue. Knowing my parents loved the children eased the pain of what I was determined to do. Their anguish over my decision would be overshadowed by the fact they would have Rosella and Brian to be a permanent part of their lives and they would lavish them with love. My sweet babies would eat well and be dressed and cared for just as I was during my childhood. No child could have a better upbringing.

Leaving the kitchen of our small apartment, I went to the children's room and packed as many of their clothes and belongings I felt I could carry. Taking too many things would raise suspicion and I didn't want anything to stop my plans. I'd thought of nothing else since Bill was led away by the officers. There was no other option. Surely mother would come back and get the rest of the children's belongings once she realized what had happened.

Waves of sorrow swept over me as I considered the grief my parents would feel when I was gone. Despair flooded my thoughts, but I brushed it aside, steeling myself against doubts that I was doing the right thing. For a fleeting moment, I held my hands on my stomach with thoughts of the baby growing in my womb. Angry with myself at the tears coursing down my face, I fought to squelch the sorrow that overshadowed my decision. Grabbing a towel, I wiped my face. I had to be resolute. The fact I was carrying our third child magnified the hopelessness of my situation. I would be unable to care for or provide for my children. It was just too much; I would finish gathering their things, take the children to my parents' home and then take my life. Fighting tears, I headed out the door with Rosella and Brian.

My ever-trusting parents didn't question my explanation that I wasn't feeling well and needed rest, asking if they would keep the children overnight. Normally very open and honest with them, I buried the hurt and shame I felt beneath my feelings of hopelessness.

I was sure that mother readily accepted my reason considering the events of the day. Her soothing voice offered exactly what I knew she would offer.

"Honey, you know we're here for you. You don't need to worry. Dad and I will take care of the kids if you decide to try to find a little job. But whatever you decide, we will see that you and the children are taken care of. You do know that, don't you?"

The concern on my mother's face came close to stopping me in my tracks. I wished I could just crawl up in mother's lap like I had as a young girl and cry away my hurt. But life was no longer that simple. There were my children to care for, another one on the way that would limit any option to work and provide for them.

Steeling myself against collapsing in mother's arms, I forced a smile and whispered, "I know, Mom, I know, and I appreciate your saying that. I do depend on you both and do need your help with the children."

Kissing my babies, holding them so tight Rosella protested, I released them and left, heading toward the Cedar River. It was March of 1961. The river in Waterloo, Iowa was at flood stage. Melting ice further north had caused the banks to overflow.

Parking my old beat up Chevy at the entrance of a bridge, I sat overwhelmed with grief and wept. Tasting the salt of my tears, I grabbed a handkerchief and dried my face. It wasn't lack of courage to throw myself into the swirling river below that caused me to hesitate. Fear of plunging to my death in the cold water was much less than the fear I had of being without Bill and unable to provide for my children.

Determined, I exited the car, inching my way down the mossy slope leading to the river's edge.

Wrapping my worn coat around me, I peered into the dark, murky water that would be my grave. It seemed to beckon me, offering to swallow both me and my unborn child along with all my worries and distress.

A slab of rock protruded out of the hillside, I sat down, considering whether or not to remove my coat and shoes. The question seemed ridiculous, considering what I was about to do. I looked heavenward, and the stars in the night sky seemed to blink their approval at my decision. It was time.

Standing to my feet, I was suddenly aware of a man approaching from my right side. The air was chilly. He wore a long coat and hat. Inexplicably I was not alarmed by his presence nor did I feel any fear of this stranger as he drew closer.

He smiled and touched my shoulder.

"Deanna, you don't want to do this."

Shocked that he knew my name, I scarcely took notice of what he'd said.

He repeated the same words, adding, "You have no right to take your own life or the life of the child growing inside of you."

His tone wasn't harsh, but authoritative. His smile was kind and his eyes showed compassion. His gaze was not offensive, but it seemed he was looking deep within my soul.

Melting in tears, bewildered by the words and manner of the man, I accepted his arm as he offered it, more in comfort than support.

With more words of encouragement and a compelling smile, the gentleman patted my arm, turned and walked away. My eyes were clouded with tears as I tried to focus, looking to see in what direction he was going. I considered following him and asking him how he knew me, how he knew my thoughts and plans to end my life. How did he know I was pregnant? I had only just recently told Bill; I hadn't yet told my parents. As I turned to call after him, he was gone. His quick exit had no explanation. There was no way he could have disappeared from sight so quickly.

The obvious angelic visitation was a turning point in my faith. I'd always been taught of Christ's love and that I should serve Him. However, the turmoil and discouraging life I'd been living with Bill for the past several years had taken me down a path of depression and despair. I'd reached the point of no hope. Inexplicably the brief visit with the stranger at the riverbank pulled me out of that abyss of hopelessness.

I left the riverbank, still without answers to how I could cope with Bill's incarceration and the care of three children. However, I now possessed a resolve, a determination within that no matter what lay in my path going forward, I would do what was right and trust God to see me through the difficult days ahead.

With the help and encouragement of my mother and father, I was able to survive. Bill spent eleven months in the psychiatric ward before finally being transferred to the State Penitentiary.

Day after day, somehow our needs were met. I got a job and worked as long as possible before our third child was born. Mother cared for Brian and Rosella, helping us get through what would otherwise have been an impossible time.

I did not waver in praying each day and night for Bill. With my parents' help, we conspired as to what we could do to see about getting an earlier release for him.

Hiring an attorney, we consistently worked toward that end. Amazingly, after a little over two years of imprisonment, Bill was released with his sentence reduced to a five-year probation. With this miracle, I had hope that I would see my prayers answered for a change in Bill's behavior.

I never told Bill or my parents how close I had come to taking my life and the life of my unborn child. It wasn't until many years later that I shared that "angelic visit" with my husband.

Much to the surprise of the local Sheriff, Bill got a job and kept his appointments with his probation officer. For a time he was sober, but that didn't last long. Going back to heavy drinking, he would be gone for two or three days at a time. During those times, I had no inkling where he was or what he was doing. He would return home just long enough to check in with his PO.

With my river experience a faint memory, it became difficult to cope with Bill's behavior. There were times I wondered if it would not have been better for him to stay in prison and serve out his full sentence. It was hard not to regret working so hard to get him released from the ten-year sentence.

Nonetheless, I continued praying that things would change and that I would have a sober and present husband, that the children would have a father who would be a good example and provider.

Despite seeing no change in Bill, my encounter at the edge of the Cedar River gave me a calm assurance that God was watching over my family. The experience was so sacred, I kept it to close to my heart, ever present in my mind. This served to keep me on a path of trust and expectation that my prayers would be answered.

Chapter Ten
Bill's story continued—Suzie

Things went from bad to worse for me. It seemed impossible, but my drinking escalated. Little Angie, our third child was now two. The year was 1963. My moments of sobriety ranged from scarce to none. Addictions ruled my life and impacted my family as never before. As the children grew older, it was becoming obvious to them that their father was nothing but a drunk. The fact that I kept in good with my parole officer amazed everyone, including me.

Deanna kept praying, but saw no results to her prayers—not concerning my behavior anyway. God did meet her needs and she worked diligently taking care of the children by herself.

One day Mother Kropp called from Colorado with an urgent message. It just so happened that I was at home that day—a rare occurrence for me—and I took the call. She explained that my little sister Suzie, now 25 years old, was gravely ill at a hospital in Cheyenne, Wyoming.

She said that Suzie was not expected to live and was asking for me. That little girl meant the world to me so I immediately began packing. Things were getting a little hot for me in Beloit anyway, but my main motivation was seeing Suzie before she died. She, after all, was the one bright spot in my childhood with the Kropps. Even though we were both adopted and from different birth parents, I considered her my baby sister and I loved her dearly.

"I'll hitchhike to Wyoming," I succinctly informed Deanna.

"No, you won't," she argued. "You'll end up getting arrested and land back in the penitentiary. I'll drive you to Cheyenne."

"That bucket of bolts you call a car will never make it," I mocked as I continued to pack.

Ignoring my remark, Deanna packed her own bag, then called her mother to take care of the children. Piling into her dilapidated vehicle, we dropped the kids off and headed to Wyoming.

Arriving about eight o'clock the next evening, we were both amazed that the automobile had held up and we had made it. How is beyond me. I was too ignorant to realize it, but despite my horrific life, there had been one miraculous appointment after another throughout.

I was shocked when I saw my precious baby sister. Her face was swollen twice its normal size. She was dying from cancer of the kidneys. She'd outlived the doctor's prognosis at her birth by twenty years.

The Kropps were exhausted. They had been sitting with Suzie all night and day. I knew they were beyond tired. They reported that Suzie had been in a coma for about three days. I asked them if I could sit with her. They reluctantly agreed and left me there alone with her. Weary from the drive, Deanna had gone to the hotel nearby where we'd paid for a room.

I paced back and forth in Suzie's hospital room. I couldn't stand seeing her the way she was. One thing for sure, I needed a drink and bad. Held there by the sight of my little sister barely breathing in that hospital bed, I didn't leave.

At about ten o'clock that night, Suzie opened her eyes. When she realized I was in the room with her, tears began coursing down her cheeks.

She said, "You know, Bill, Jesus promised me enough time to talk to you about Him before I die. I'm worried about your soul and where you'll spend eternity. I'm getting ready to go and be with Jesus. I'm looking forward to being free from pain and distress. He's waiting for me with outstretched arms."

With great difficulty, she began to unfold the vast plan of salvation that Jesus offered me.

"Bill, you need to get saved. You need to confess your sins, allow Jesus to wash you and make you clean with His blood that He shed on the Cross of Calvary."

I began to get angry. "I am saved!" I shouted, then remembering I was in a hospital, lowered my voice as I continued to argue and repeat again, "I am saved."

Suzie smiled weakly, "You know, Bill, Mom and Dad have been telling me what's going on in your life and you're not being honest with me."

Even though I grew angrier, I suppressed it because of her condition. I could almost see and hear Shorty Mills talking to me about Jesus, talking to me about giving my life over to Him. I gritted my teeth, I was so agitated.

Hanging my head, I listened to her take every bit of strength she had to pray for me. She prayed for my soul. With all that she was suffering, her main concern was for me. She kept insisting I needed to surrender my life to Christ, accept His salvation and deliverance. She told me about a loving Heavenly Father who sent His only Son, Jesus, to die on a cruel cross. Struggling to breathe, she used what little breath she had to explain that Christ was the perfect sacrifice for the sins of the world—that no matter what I'd done, He loved me and would forgive me if I asked Him.

That little girl prayed, calling my name out before God, in Jesus' name, asking Him to show me His love and power to forgive and change me. I'll never forget the fervor with which she prayed for me, and then she lapsed into unconsciousness again.

I felt the weight of conviction so strong. I couldn't wait until Mom and Dad Kropp returned. They had promised to be back at eight o'clock the next morning. Barely acknowledging them when they entered the hospital room, I literally ran from there and began hitting the bars.

When my money was depleted, I went into drugstores. I stole bottles of rubbing alcohol, then stole loaves of bread. I found a coffee can in the trash in an alley where I poured the rubbing alcohol through the bread to take the fire out of it so I could get it down.

I drank and drank and couldn't get drunk. I was miserable with stomach cramps. Then hallucinations began. That scared me. I went to the hotel room where Deanna was staying in Cheyenne. I'm surprised I could find it, I was in such a state. She could see that I was a mess but didn't know what set me off.

I told her, "Suzie talked to me about Jesus and praying and talking about crazy stuff."

Deanna looked at me and said, "Bill, I think you're under conviction."

I just looked at her with blood-shot eyes. I'm sure I looked like a wild man. I didn't know what she meant. The only conviction I knew about was standing in front of a judge. I didn't need my wife or anyone else talking to me about conviction. I'd been arrested and convicted of crimes, sentenced and served time more than any one person should. Conviction was something of which I wanted no part.

Deanna, aware I was confused, explained, "Bill, you're under the conviction of the Holy Spirit."

She made me furious. Her words lit a fuse that erupted like dynamite in my head. My temper had always been violent, but I'd never lashed out at her with physical abuse. I hit her and knocked her down on the floor. Realizing how out of control I was, I ran from the hotel and kept drinking, and drinking more. I still couldn't get drunk, I was a raving lunatic—beside myself—why couldn't I get drunk, why couldn't I just pass out and…

When the DT's started, I began seeing spiders coming up out of the cracks in the sidewalks. I knew then the thing I feared most was death. Running back to the hotel, I told Deanna what was happening to me. My stomach cramps had escalated and were so bad I couldn't stand up. I continued hallucinating. Looking at my body, I could see every muscle flexing back and forth. Panic-stricken, I begged Deanna to do something to help me.

She said, "I'll take you to find a church. I'll find the local Salvation Army."

I was so sick and hurting, I didn't care. I said, "Take me somewhere, anywhere.

Chapter Eleven
Encounter With Christ

Inquiring where the Salvation Army was located, Deanna steered in that direction with me trying to hang on to my sanity. Wild-eyed, doubled over in pain, I was a sight to behold. I couldn't have been coherent. I'd never experienced anything like this.

As we rounded the corner, within sight of the Salvation Army building, Deanna commented, "That man getting into the car might be a Captain." She was familiar enough with the organization to recognize the dress uniform that would be worn by the "Captain."

We were at a stoplight. In my present physical state, I don't know how I managed it, but, I jumped out of the car and began running down the street, screaming and hollering for him to stop. It's good that he didn't see or hear me as he probably would have ducked back into his car and run for his life from the mad man approaching. He stopped, not because he heard me, but because he had forgotten his hat.

Noticing me out of the corner of his eye, he stopped. I'm sure he thought I was insane, but then he no doubt had seen others as worked up as I was.

I doubt he'd seen anyone, however, as out of control as me.

Seeing my state of mind, he graciously agreed to take me to his office to talk to me. But he started to talk about the same things Suzie talked about Jesus and salvation. I was very uncomfortable and nervous. The man was smart enough to know what was happening to me. He had taken me into his office, a place of authority. He could see I was feeling trapped just as if sitting in front of a judge or a person connected to law enforcement. So he wisely asked me to follow him out of his office and into the sanctuary.

The church was small with a red carpet. Sitting me down on the front pew, he sat down beside me with his wife who he had invited to visit with Deanna and me. I was bent over, still cramped up.

He said, "Bill, you need to come over, kneel at this altar, and pray."

I said, "Okay, I'll do anything you want me to do." My compliance was strictly because of how much I was suffering. I had to get relief; I'd try anything.

So I got up off the pew and never made it to the altar. I fell on the floor, cramped up into a ball and began to vomit and vomit and vomit some more. Rolling in my own filth, smelling terrible, I recall the Captain coming over, and laying hands on me. He asked me to pray.

I said, "I don't know how to pray." The whole situation was so surreal, I looked at him and said, "You mean this prayer: 'Now I lay me down to sleep, I pray the Lord my soul to keep…' You mean that prayer?"

He looked at me with eyes full of compassion and said, "Bill, you talk to Jesus just like you're talking to me."

"But I don't know what to say," I stammered, still slobbering and reeking of vomit.

I was not very coherent in my state of mental and physical anguish but cognizant enough to wonder how the man could stand to be beside me. I knew I was repulsive, yet he looked down at me, smiled and said, "Just tell Him you're sorry."

I remember to this day, exactly what I said. I blurted out, "Jesus, if you'll get this monkey off my back, I'll do whatever you want me to do."

Inexplicably, my stomach cramps stopped immediately; my DT's vanished. I got up off that floor. I felt like I was walking on air. I wasn't sure what had happened.

The Captain explained it to me, and Deanna explained it to me and she prayed with me all the way home. Of course, I had a hard time praying. I didn't know how to pray.

I remember saying, "Okay, Jesus, if you're who you say you are, I'll do this, and this, and that…" like a babe in Christ—and I was definitely that.

Looking over at Deanna I said, "Honey, when we get back home, I have a lot of things to face. There's a warrant out for my arrest. I could very easily be sent back to prison to serve out the balance of my ten-year sentence. You know I've broken the terms of my probation and I'll have to face the music." I couldn't help but wonder if she would be willing to stick with me once again as she always had.

She was well aware, and I saw her lips move in prayer, even as I laid out the reality of the situation.

The truth was that the Sheriff was looking for me in Waterloo, Iowa. That is where we were going to have to go as we had no other option. Deanna's parents were there and we would be able to stay with them. There was no running. It didn't even enter my mind. Why did I suddenly feel an overpowering, inexplicable peace and assurance about facing the Sheriff? I can only say it was the peace that Christ offers, a tranquility of mind and soul that overrides and surpasses all else.

I said, "I've got to go see the Sheriff."

He was the probation officer back then as well as the Sheriff. When I walked into his office, he had no choice but to lock me up.

I began telling him about my experience in Cheyenne. I told him in my own ignorant way, "I've got this 'Jesus thing', and I got saved, and I don't drink anymore." He just looked at me. I'm sure he'd heard everything. But this was the first time he'd ever heard anything like this from my lips.

Unbelievably—but realize, this is just how God works—he came in the next day and said, "I don't know why I'm doing this—you have done nothing but give me fits for the last year and a half—but I'm going to let you out, and you go find a job and report back here every hour on the hour."

That's exactly what I did. I'd hunt for a job, when an hour had passed, I was back on the jailhouse steps, reporting in. This went on for about twelve hours. I finally went into his office and told him, "You know I can't find a job if I have to stop and report back to you every hour."

A few days passed with this routine continuing. He came in one morning and I was sitting on the steps as always.

"Oh, you're still here," he commented. "I figured you'd have run off again by now."

He let me go, and I found a job. Deanna and I started going to church and I kept witnessing to that Sheriff.

I now saw the miraculous hand of God work in the heart of this skeptical Sheriff, the mercy and love of God on my behalf was blowing his mind as well as mine. I couldn't understand it; I knew I didn't deserve it and wondered if it was God's love for my wife and kids that compelled Him to give me favor and so many miracles. Because now I began to think of everything He'd kept me from and seen me through since my life began. I just couldn't yet wrap my mind around the fact that God really loved me, miserable wretch of humanity that I had always been.

Chapter Twelve
Finding My Father

Not knowing who my father was always bothered me. It was a hidden longing—not something I thought about all the time, mostly when other people talked about their relationships with their fathers. Growing up, if I missed having a father/son relationship, I didn't dwell on the fact.

Genealogy is a big deal to some people. People like to follow their roots and discover where they came from. Some folk make a life-long career of it. Except for what my mother told me, I didn't have a clue where to begin, and it would be useless to engage in a search. My mother wasn't able to give me a name. Her telling me that he was a Captain in the army meant nothing without a name.

A father usually plays such an important role in a young boy's life. An attentive father is a mentor, giving life lessons by example. Work ethic, how to treat others, all goes into the shaping of his psyche, his personality, and his behavior. It is by example, rather than lecture that the boy learns. Seeing how the dad treats his wife, how he provides for his family, and how he loves his son is vital to molding the boy into a young man of good character.

Having a nurturing dad in no way insures success in life, however, it does give a better chance of following the right path. A father's steps help mark the path that is best to travel. His guidance also gives direction in distinguishing dangerous detours that draw away from the best roads to take.

I'm not blaming my behavior on the lack of a biological father in my life. Knowing his name and finding him would not be productive if he didn't want me or if he was not a man of good character.

Mr. Kropp was a good provider for the household where I was raised. However, he spent little time nurturing me. He did save my life more than once just by his presence when Mrs. Kropp seemed bent on killing me.

He was the only dad I knew, and I did appreciate him—but I always knew he wasn't my father. I knew I wasn't loved like a son, and that emptiness haunted me throughout my life even though I wasn't fully aware of the void it caused.

The day I found my father was the most amazing day of my life. Nothing can compare to the thrill I felt when I realized he not only loved me, but loved me unconditionally. Despite the fact I was now a grown man, he embraced me with comfort and compassion that left me breathless.

Aware that He would provide for me, give me direction and guidance even though I was no longer a young boy was amazing to me. Now cognizant that he had always loved me, sought me out, been waiting for me to find him—I could only weep in His presence.

The fact that He had every answer to any problem I faced, that He was willing to listen to me any time of the day or night—it was incomprehensible. If only I'd found Him sooner. I was now in the position to feel regret for most of my life.

You might wonder how in the world I found Him without knowing His name. Well, the truth is He knew my name. He reached out for me when I didn't know His name. He'd sent out several messengers to lead me in the right direction to find Him.

One was Shorty Mills, my friend that fed the ammo to the fifty-caliber machine gun I fired on Pork Chop Hill in Korea. There were a couple others in that pit I was thrown into at the Korean POW camp. They talked about my Father and tried to help me find Him when I was too immersed in myself to listen. Then there was sweet Suzie. She knew my Father all along.

Even though we were birthed by different mothers, Suzie knew my real Father. Before she breathed her last breath, she took every bit of her strength to tell me about Him. Still blinded to whom He was, not able to understand, I ran from the truth.

But He didn't give up on me. When I was at my worst, drunk, hateful, deep in sin, He loved me and He stood with arms outstretched, waiting for me to finally realize who He was. He was there all the time.

Yeah, if you haven't realized yet, I have a Father, a Heavenly Father. He is everything to me, my provider, my salvation, my deliverer, my healer, my strength. He's the one Shorty Mills told me about: *For God so loved the world that He gave His only begotten Son, that whosoever believes in Him will not perish, but have everlasting life.* John 3:16

When I repented of my sin and turned my back on the old me—the vile, addicted, miserable lump of humanity—I became a Child of God! What a revelation to know I now had a Father, one who loved me despite of who I was, who I had been. He reached down and picked me up out of my hopeless existence and gave me the key to His Kingdom. I was now His son. As His son, I now was an heir and joint-heir with Jesus Christ!

Looking back over the jumbled mess of my life, I began to come to the realization that He not only was waiting patiently for me to wake up to who He was, but He was always mindful of me. All the miracles, all the strange occurrences—these were no coincidences. It didn't just happen that a hobo and bum were on that freight train I hopped in Iowa. It was not a fluke that the judge offered me the army rather than federal prison or that Shorty Mills was in the gunner nest with me. Nor was it coincidental that my grandmother rescued me from bleeding to death, entering the house just in time. The respite I received during my stay with Grandma and Grandpa Brown was also, I believe, the hand of God sparing my life.

Being at home when the call came that Suzie was dying was unusual. It was during a time that I was seldom at home and never sober. But I was that time. The Salvation Army Captain forgetting his hat—I could go on and don't remember all of the times I benefited by the "perfect timing" of my Heavenly Father who knew what I needed and when.

Bowing before Him, I wept in humility that the great God of Heaven, my Father, regarded me as His son—worthy of redemption only because of the sacrifice of Christ. My "Abba Father" who I now could cry out to anytime as my "Daddy".

Chapter Thirteen
The Call

From the moment of my conversion, I felt a stirring in the core of my being. We joined the Salvation Army and began working for them. God's call became stronger with the passing of each day. I was teaching a nine-year-old boys' class. Since I was unable to read or write, Deanna would help me put my thoughts together.

It was a proud day for the new and improved Bill Kropp when I received my Salvation Army uniform. I wore this uniform in the middle of July. It was hot and the conference we were attending in Des Moines, Iowa was boring. I realized later that Jesus didn't want me there; He took me out of that meeting. I went looking for a coffee shop. Stumbling over some garbage, I noticed a guy between two trashcans. There was a gunnysack over his face and his bare feet were sticking out. I wasn't sure if he was dead or alive. I pulled the sack from his face; it was obvious he'd been severely beaten.

I was looking down at him when God spoke to me, **"*But for my grace, this would be you.*"** I reached down and picked the man up and we stumbled out of that alley. He fell against my white shirt and got blood all over me. As we continued struggling down the street, a man joined us. I hadn't noticed him before, but he appeared and spoke to me, ***"Bill, this is what I'm calling you to do."***

I argued, "I can't do this; I can't read or write. What do you want me to do?"

His answer was simple: ***"I want you to lead people like you're leading this man right now. You're leading him to victory and to help."***

I didn't stop arguing back and forth, back and forth. When we got to the door of the shelter, the mysterious man's final answer to me was: ***"Through Christ, all things are possible."***

In a fit of anger—my temper was still alive and well—I said, "Okay, I'll do what you want me to do." The man following along with us turned and was gone.

I went to my preacher at the Salvation Army and told him in detail my experience in the alley. His comment reinforced my own argument as he said, "Bill, it's going to be a struggle; you're on parole and let me ask you, you can't read or write, can you?"

Fortunately that was not the end of things. I knew the encounter with either an angel or the Lord Himself was real and something I could not walk away from. A godly man stepped forward to help me. He tutored me about the requirements for ministry credentials. This man was Sterling Poling, the local Salvation Army officer's son-in-law. His compassion and patience with me was amazing. He worked tirelessly, getting me through my studies.

You see, my Father was still looking out for me. He always makes a way when there isn't one.

There was a test several pages long to get into Bible College with the Salvation Army. My friend took on the task of guiding me through the process.

His plan was like this. He said, "I'll read the Scripture and the question to you. You give me the answer and I'll write it down for you."

I passed with an 82%. I still hesitated to attend Bible College. I was 27 years old—I would be the oldest one in our class. Hesitation kept me back for over a year. I still couldn't read. That fact eroded any confidence I had.

One night, while sound asleep, God woke me up. How did I know it was God? Well for one thing, He spoke to me—and what followed made me aware that it had to be God.

"*Pick up your Bible!*"

His clarion voice was unmistakable. But my argumentative response was typical. "You know I can't read."

"*Open your Bible!*"

Aware that this was not a suggestion, I complied. My mind swirled with amazement as my heart soared—I could read every word. I woke up Deanna and said, "Listen." I turned to the book of John and started reading. She broke down and cried. I joined with her, and through my tears was able to read, *In the beginning was the Word, and the Word was with God, and the Word was God, the same was in the beginning with God. All things were made by Him, and without Him was not anything made that was made...*

I couldn't stop reading. Wiping my tears, I continued. Realize, reader, I had not memorized Scripture; this was a miracle straight from the hand of God. I could read. That was a huge hurdle conquered. Deanna would be able to help me write and spell. My Father was at work teaching me what I'd never learned and was unable to learn on my own.

That Sunday I testified about what God accomplished in my mind. Everyone was so moved by the miraculous, several people came forward and committed their lives to Christ, repenting of sin, determined to serve the Lord. Everything God does has an exponential result. I wonder of those saved in that service—how many lives they touched as they testified of the saving power of the Cross of Christ. That's just how God works. He taught me to read in a moment of time—that testimony changed the lives of others and they went on to reach more. Talk about a pyramid scheme—except it's no scheme—it's the powerful way God works.

Well, we went into Bible College and completed our first year. It was a struggle for me. I could now read and write, but couldn't comprehend. The history of my education was sketchy at best. While I attended through the eighth grade, truancy and never doing assignments was the reason I could not read or write.

Passing the tests was the insurmountable mountain for me. Deanna would hardly crack a book and make an A. On top of my lack of academic skills, I still carried with me the horrors of war. The gut wrenching nightmares were no longer as frequent, however I could not be around fireworks or loud popping noises. These things sent me back to the battlefield with all the smells, sights, and sounds of death.

I recall walking through the long hall of the housing facility at the college. Some smart aleck chose that exact time to set off some firecrackers. My reflex was instant. I was ready to fight and know I was held at bay by the mercy and grace of God. That could have been the end of my Bible College education and my ability to follow the call on my life.

Somehow I made it through that first year.

At Christmas we went back home for the two-week vacation from school. I went over to see the Sheriff. I was really proud of my uniform. I was the first Salvation Army cadet accepted into the program that was on parole with a five-year probation.

Sharing my testimony with that Sheriff, I told him in detail about what happened with Suzie and how I drank my way to speak to the Salvation Army Captain. Seeing tears in Sheriff Jack's eyes, I continued to tell him of the many miracles God had given Deanna and me.

Before I left him, he said the sinner's prayer. His glorious salvation is such a wonderful reflection of the power of God—turning me from a filthy criminal, uneducated, rejected, and unloved, into someone who could lead my parole officer to the foot of the Cross of Calvary.

Chapter Fourteen
Ministry

We went back to Bible College for the second year. It was a little easier, but I still had to put everything into it, and with Deanna's help, made it through the required courses for credentials.

After spending the summer in a ministry assignment, we were worried for the finances needed to provide for our three children for the coming school year. They were in public school and we didn't have funds to get them school supplies or decent school clothes. As children do, they had grown out of all their clothes from the year before. We were living in Chicago so besides regular clothing, they also needed warm coats.

Our summer ministry had been in Hutchinson, Kansas with on-site training for three months. We traveled by train from Chicago to Hutchinson in June, and returned to Chicago in late August by train. Upon arriving back at Bible School in Chicago, we discovered two huge boxes sitting in our apartment. They were marked from Fargo, North Dakota.

They were filled with brand new school clothes, shoes, school supplies, and winter coats, boots and everything the children needed—all in their correct sizes. A lady in Fargo called the Bible School requesting our name and all the names and sizes of our children. She told that she'd had a dream about us. God told her to call the school for the information and send the boxes. She and her church put everything together. Needless to say, we were thrilled and so grateful. It was when we wrote to thank them that they told us all the circumstances of how God spoke to them to buy the items and send them to us. It was one of many times we saw the hand of God working and letting us know He was with us, that we were doing what He'd called us to do and that He would supply all our needs.

It was beyond humbling to be credentialed for ministry with the Salvation Army. My experience with the other army that impacted my life resulted in a dishonorable discharge. Now transformed by the renewing power of Christ through the Cross, I was a new creature and in a new army with a high rank of royalty—as child of the King of Kings.

The first place of ministry we were assigned was in St. Louis, Missouri. It was a storefront facility with a congregation of about five people. Because of the mandate I'd received from God to lead the addicted and hurting to Him, a fire burned within me that compelled me to reach out to the lost in that area. After about a year and a half, our number expanded to about 75 people.

The "Army" then transferred us to Springfield, Illinois. During our seven years there, I received the powerful experience of being filled with the Holy Ghost. By this time we had two more children: Kevin and Ann.

It is remarkable how God uses people. He had already introduced so many into my troubled life that were instrumental in taking me from a destructive path: my sister Suzie, Shorty Mills, the two fellows who prayed for and quoted Scripture to all of us in the POW pit, Deanna, the Captain, and others.

I recall one woman, Lila DeLong. She had four children. We would take the bus and pick her kids up for Sunday school and church. We found them with dirty faces, not dressed properly. We would wash them and get them dressed. Mom was sleeping, as she was a barmaid and worked nights. God makes it clear in His Word that we are to reach out to and "suffer" or allow the little children to come. Ministering to children, especially those who are neglected, even unloved and unwanted, is one that brings results and pleases God!

A Sunday school contest was held with a bike as the prize. Lila's children wore her down, begging her to come to church with them so they could win the bicycle. She came once, then again. She was being drawn by the Spirit of God.

The Holy Spirit got a hook in her jaw and reeled her in. She was gloriously saved. The change that took place in her was astronomical. Lila was not the kind of person who did things in a mediocre way. She plunged headlong into church activities. She became one of the driving forces of the growth of the church. If you wanted something done, you looked to Lila. Her enthusiasm, dedication, and commitment to serving Christ put the rest of us to shame. During the course of time she met some people who were Pentecostal.

Hungry for a deeper experience with God, she listened to their explanations and their reference to Acts 2:4. I warned her that these people were weird. Personally, I was scared to death of them. I'd heard all the stories about "Holy Rollers," "Pew Jumpers," and more.

As was her custom, Lila always found herself at the altar at the close of every service. Crying out to God one Sunday evening, she began praying in another language. She was speaking in tongues.

Afterward she approached me and said, "Pastor, I'll have to find another church. I know you don't approve of speaking in tongues, but it's real, and I cannot deny the power of the Holy Spirit."

My response was sincere. "I don't understand it, but I know you, and that you're genuine. That's all that counts." Truthfully, I didn't want to lose a good worker. She would be irreplaceable in the church.

What continued to work on me was seeing her as she worked with alcoholics and transients. The love, compassion, and wisdom she poured out convinced me she had something powerful. I still couldn't come to grips with the "tongue talking" though. She seemed stable and I hoped it would be a passing phase with her.

What sealed the deal with me was when we became acquainted with the *Bobby Kay Singers*. They too were Pentecostal. We continue a lasting friendship with them to this day.

Borrowing chairs from us, they explained they would be ministering at the State Fair. Curious to hear them, we went to listen. They were singing old country Gospel songs. What impressed me the most were their expressions of love. They didn't know much about the Bible—in fact, were a little rough around the edges. They would not have passed the litmus test of proper etiquette and liturgy in most churches.

By then, I was learning more and more each day. We were good for each other. They gave me a book, *They Speak With Other Tongues* by John L. Sherrill.

For a while it collected dust on my dresser. Still convinced "speaking in tongues" may be of the devil, I wasn't sure I should even have it in the house. A month or two later, God woke me up in the night. He's pretty good at that—guess He knows that's the best time to get my attention.

He said, ***"Read the Book!"***

I didn't argue with Him. I knew I wouldn't win. So I sat there and read the book. By the time I was done, my curiosity to learn more was piqued.

There was one amazing account in the book of a miraculous rescue from a cannibalistic tribe in Africa. This incident occurred at the time the continent was referred to as *The White Man's Grave*. A missionary by the name of H. B. Garlock was surrounded by a tribe known to be cannibalistic. The miraculous account in Sherrill's book told how Garlock stood boldly and began to speak in a language he himself did not understand. He later learned he had preached the Gospel in the tribal tongue under the anointing of the Holy Spirit. The entire village surrendered their lives to Christ.

I was amazed, not just by that particular account, but by everything recorded in the book. The result was I promised to go with the *Bobby Kay Singers* to Chicago to a Katherine Kuhlman meeting.

She preached, gave the altar call, and then gave a call for those who wished to receive the Holy Spirit. Nothing happened to me. The meeting was fine, but I was unimpressed. I figured I should feel something akin to a lightening bolt from Heaven taking control of my speech.

They also had a youth meeting that I attended. It was packed; there were no seats except a few right up front by the platform. The fellow preaching was on fire. He preached about the Baptism of the Holy Spirit, but said very little about "tongues." I was glad. It was the "tongues" that frightened me. Well, he finished with prayer and nothing happened to me although others around me were in worship and speaking a Heavenly language. I felt nothing.

I was ready to get up from praying. My plan was to walk out. I was disappointed. Even though I was feeling uneasy about the experience, I had wanted something to happen. I was certainly no stranger to God doing the unexpected and the miraculous in my life.

A Baptist minister in clerical garb and a Catholic priest in high collar approached me. There was quite a mix of denominations represented in the meeting. I, however, had left my Salvation Army uniform back home—I didn't want to embarrass my organization or myself. They began to explain to me what was going on around me. We were all sitting on the floor because I hadn't gotten up from my praying position.

They began to pray for me, and I joined in, praying. When the Holy Spirit came on me, I sat there on that floor, rocking back and forth like a seal, clapping my hands and saying, "It's real, it's real!" It's one thing to look askance at someone else's experience or even question an account written in a book you read, but when you personally experience the power of the Holy Spirit filling every fiber of your being, there is no denying the reality of the experience of "being filled with the Spirit evidenced by speaking in other tongues."

I no longer questioned if it was from the Lord—it could not be denied that the power of the Holy Spirit overshadowing me could not be contained. I erupted, speaking in tongues. Yes, I now knew this Pentecostal experience was real!

We headed for home on Saturday. I was prepared with my Sunday sermon. It was written down, word for word. I could read now and that's how I put my messages together, delivering them by reading. Now, filled with the Holy Spirit, this would really be good. That's what I told myself. I was ready to "knock the congregation on their heels".

But when the time came, I could not get up to preach. Looking to Deanna I said, "I don't know what's wrong, but I can't preach." She bailed me out, which was the norm for her and she did a great job.

I went to the prayer room, not knowing what was wrong. I was full of the Holy Spirit, yet when I opened my Bible it seemed someone had stolen it. Shouldn't this be better, easier now that I'd received the infilling of the Spirit?

The Lord spoke to me, ***"Open your Bible again."***

Obediently I did so and found myself in the 14th chapter of John. The Lord said, ***"Preach on that."***

For 45 minutes I preached without a note. Fourteen people came forward and accepted Christ as their Savior that night. God is amazing. It did not go without my notice that the fourteenth chapter of John produced 14 new souls into the Kingdom of God. I love it when He adds little touches to His mighty workings. He certainly has His own way of doing things, and I love it when nothing goes the way I think it will, but instead according to His will and way!

Our Sunday school began to grow. From 80 we mushroomed to 800 and were bursting out of the walls. The joy of the Lord erupted in a way that people seemed to be drawn to the services. I honestly knew it had nothing to do with me or any programs we were implementing; it was the power of the Holy Spirit drawing people off the street, bringing them in to hear the Gospel message. They were changed, delivered from their addictions, and began to then minister to and bring in others.

One Sunday morning, we had the *Bobby Kay Singers* come to minister. A Salvation Army Commander came to visit from St. Louis. Word was out that we were "Floor Buffers." If you wanted your floors buffed, just call us—we'd roll on the floor and buff them. It was another name for "Holy Rollers."

Rumors floated in all directions and reached his ears. Had he come to "spy out" the land? Probably so. When he arrived, he was shocked that we were so full. There were no vacant seats. He was standing when someone noticed, got up, and offered him theirs.

Following my preaching, as was the custom, I gave an altar call. People flooded the altar. One of the *Bobby Kay Singers* knelt to pray. The commander laid his hand on her. He, no doubt, thought she had come for salvation, but she had just come to pray. All of a sudden, she broke forth speaking in tongues. Cringing, I was sure I'd had it! I'd secretly hoped there would be no such manifestation while he was there.

Gathering at the shelter later for lunch, the Commander ate with Deanna and me, passing the time with small talk. When he was ready to leave, he called me aside; I knew this was it. Breathing a prayer that I would be true to my experience and yet find favor with the Commander, I followed him to his car.

As we walked, for the longest time nothing was said by either of us. The Commander finally looked at me and said, "Bill, I don't know what you're doing, but whatever it is, keep doing it."

I didn't need to be told twice. I had great respect for the man as we shook hands that day. He certainly was aware that something good was going on in our church.

Eventually we ended up in St. Joseph, Missouri. It was due to the process of moving officers. My name came up and we were sent to the town famous for the Pony Express and the place where Jesse James met his end. The year we moved was 1971.

Now known as Captain Kropp, I continued with the call God placed on my life. Again, God gives little touches to our lives, letting us know He's there with the monumental miracles—like changing a drunken bum into a Salvation Army Captain. I just love it when He puts the "frosting" on the cake. My mother had told me my biological father was an Army Captain. Well, maybe he was, maybe he wasn't—only God knows. I'm not sure that my mother knew. The irony, God's irony, was now I was a Captain in an Army—the Salvation Army.

Meeting with pastors, bishops, nuns and Christian businessmen and women, we soon found ourselves forming a group called *One In The Spirit*. The bond of being "one in the Spirit" united us as we held non-denominational meetings at different locations each month. It was a time of making lifelong friendships, encouraging one another in fulfilling our individual calls to minister.

We also became involved in a movement known as *Full Gospel Businessmen*. It was at one of those dinner meetings that I first learned of Deanna's amazing testimony at the Cedar River bank in Waterloo, Iowa. Remember, I was incarcerated when that happened and once I got out of prison our lives were so hectic she'd never shared the story with me. Hearing her tell that experience brought me to tears as I thought of the agony I'd put my wonderful wife through because of my callous and selfish actions.

Amazed once again at the hand of God on my life and my family, I felt humbled and unworthy of His marvelous love, mercy, and grace! What a Father I have. He was always there—when I took no thought of Him, He loved me. When I didn't have the good sense to be a father and provider for my family, He still loved me. That love drew me, a worthless piece of humanity until I surrendered to Him at the foot of the Cross.

Chapter Fifteen
Ministry Opportunities

I love following the direction of God. He opens opportunities of ministry that would be impossible ever on my own. It's great to put Him in charge of choosing where we should go, when, how, and even the why. He sets things up, putting people in our path that will be a blessing to us or we will be a blessing to. Sometimes when we think we are being sent to "bless," the reverse takes place and we are the ones who are "blessed." The main thing to remember is that He knows what He is doing.

The different twists and turns my life took even before I surrendered to Him, I believe, were all ordered and part of drawing me to the foot of the cross. My sister, Suzie, her prayers for me, Shorty Mills who I met under the worse of circumstances, the men at the POW camp who prayed for and quoted Scriptures to us and of course, Deanna's willingness to marry a "mess" like me. All of them were divinely tuned instruments, used to bring me to the one who could mend this wounded, broken person I was.

After I achieved the distinction of being a "Captain" in the Salvation Army, I had the privilege of speaking at places other than the location where I was assigned. Traveling to the prisons in Illinois and Indiana and other states was a great opportunity I was given. Some of the facilities were where I had been incarcerated. What a thrill to stand there as a free individual, not just free from imprisonment in a state facility, but free from the bondage of alcohol and sin. Free in Christ. The men listened to me because I knew what they were going through. I'd been there; I had found the way out of a life of crime and destruction. I had the answer for them and they listened.

Now a Captain in a different army than the one I served in during the Korean War, I also was allowed to come and speak to different military groups. I'll never forget the time I went to speak to the National Guard in Springfield. Amazingly there in the audience was the same Sarge that trained me before I was sent over to Korea. He came up to me afterward, astonished as he told me, "You're certainly not the same guy I knew when you were at boot camp."

Again, I had to smile at how God sends those little touches to add to our experience. To be able to testify to that man about the miracle of a changed life was just the whipped cream and cherry on the top of a hot fudge sundae. I don't mean to trivialize the workings of God with that illustration—I just want to express it in a down to earth way.

That's just a little thing, but throughout my ministry I see the hand of God over and over again—going just a little further, doing just a little more, and always in His own perfect, finishing way. The Scripture tells us He does exceedingly and abundantly above and beyond what we can even imagine or think. And he never halfway does anything. He finishes the work He begins. When we trust Him to do so, that is. His ways are beyond our ways and are past finding out. That's why it's best to just give Him our worries, our troubles, our struggles, the things we have no control over and let Him work His best work. He will and He'll even work our failures for good.

Romans 8:28 states: *And we know, all things work for good to them that love God.* ALL things, not just some things. As we give everything to Him, He can take the worse circumstances and turn them around, not just for our good, but also for the good of those we love and care about.

I urge you to give everything to Him. He's a miracle worker. He can take a miserable drunk, a worthless mass of humanity, clean him up, change him, and set him in heavenly places with Christ.

Chapter Seventeen
Forgiveness

Bill the little unwanted, unloved, abused boy no longer existed. To say my life to the point before I entered the Salvation Army experiencing the DT's was Hell on earth is an understatement. Son of a roadhouse prostitute, what chance did I have to become a person of any worth?

My mother still in her teens, no father as part of my life—it seemed a Godsend to my mother, Margaret, when the Kropps offered to adopt me. Mrs. Kropp—always the great benefactor—taking care of my mother until I was born, taking in the little severely handicapped Suzie—she was the epitome of compassion—or so it seemed.

I quickly became the one who knew the real Mrs. Kropp. Beatings, humiliation, being locked outside in the cold, attacks that took me close to death—these were daily occurrences. My hatred for her reached the extreme.

Something happened, however, when I received forgiveness from Christ. All my sins against Him, against my wife and family, against the rules of law were wiped out in an instant because of the Cross of Calvary. I became a new creature, washed in the blood of Jesus. There's no way I can explain that miracle, only that I knew when it happened and I was never the same again.

That's when I began to realize my hatred for Mrs. Kropp could not remain a part of the fiber of my being if I wanted Christ's forgiveness of me to stand. The Biblical mandate is *forgive others if you want to be forgiven.* This is crystal clear in the eighteenth chapter of Matthew when the disciples ask Jesus how often they should forgive an offense. His answer is not what we want to hear. Jesus then goes on and talks about the servant who is forgiven a great debt, goes out free, and then takes someone by the throat that owes him a small amount. The Lord of that servant is angry and condemns the unjust servant. In Matthew 18:35, Jesus states: *So likewise shall my Heavenly Father do also unto you, if ye from your hearts forgive not everyone his brother, their trespasses.*

I was well aware that my feelings toward Mrs. Kropp had to be taken care of. My adoptive parents moved back to Indianapolis after Suzie's death. They wanted to be near Joanne, their only biological daughter and her family. We had just begun our Bible College years in Chicago.

Mr. and Mrs. Kropp began to attend church with their daughter and her family at a Seventh Day Adventist Church in Indianapolis. We could see a change taking place in Mrs. Kropp when we went to spend Christmas with them. It was our second year of Bible College. She was very loving and tender with our children, and actually seemed to be reaching out to me.

My sister, Joanne, was married to a fine Christian man who was a deacon in their church. He was a kind man of good character and was having a big impact on the elder Kropps.

Some years later they all came to visit us in our Springfield, Illinois church. This was after I had received the Pentecostal experience of being filled with the Holy Ghost according to Acts 2:4. Following the Sunday morning service where I had preached, my mother, father, sister, and brother-in-law all came forward to pray. They wanted to understand what had happened to me that caused such a dramatic and lasting change. As God melted my "mother's" heart, I too allowed the healing power of the Holy Spirit to bind up the wounds of my childhood. Without speaking definitively about the past, things were mended between her and me.

There was a specific time, however, when Mrs. Kropp was ill in the hospital. Gone was her strength and steely nature toward me. She was sick and humbled. She looked at me with tears in her eyes and asked for my forgiveness. How could I deny her? I could not. Thinking of the mercy and forgiveness of God toward me, I readily took her hand and we wept together, putting the past where it belonged—in the "Sea of God's forgetfulness."

I was made aware too that she suffered from an imbalance of hormones. Of course, as a child this was not explained to me, nor would I have understood. I don't think she realized it at the time, but it was indeed the reason for her erratic behavior, and a huge part of why she could not tolerate a little boy who was starving for love and acceptance. But thanks be to God, He is a healer of broken hearts and a restorer of families!

God did a work in their hearts and healed all the differences in doctrine. What a miracle that was. A further healing took place. It had been gradual throughout the years, but was then complete. All bitterness and animosity between Mrs. Kropp and me dissolved at the foot of the cross of Jesus Christ.

I'm confident I will see them in Heaven someday when we all gather around the throne of Christ. Joanne still lives in Indianapolis. We have the joy of visiting with her as often as we are able. Although not blood related, we are bound by something even stronger—a love for each other as brother and sister.

Epilogue

The years have brought me to the ripe old age of 80. God has not forsaken me; He's still allowing me to preach and proclaim His power and strength to this generation. (Psalm 71:18)

Deanna and I still reside in St. Joseph, Missouri. We pastor Central Assembly of God in this city and have for thirteen years as of 2016. We have no plans to step away from the call God placed on me years ago in that alley as I took a battered man to find help and shelter.

Jesus still heals the broken, binds up the deep wounds left by sin, forgives and sets free from the bondage of Satan. He did it for me, and He'll do it for you. His love compels Him!

As long as He gives me breath, I'll tell the story of Christ's sacrifice and redeeming power. He is the same yesterday, today, and forever. (Hebrews 13:8) He is still Healer, Savior, Baptizer, and Soon Coming King.

It has been our joy to take into our home, throughout our fifty years of marriage, thirty foster children, most of them teenagers. Being given the opportunity to show them love and family and a loving Jesus who is always there for them has been the greatest blessing for us. We are thrilled that a great number of these foster children accepted the Lord and many are in ministry today, serving the Lord.

We have been blessed with five biological children: Rosella Hagar, Brian Kropp, Angela Grider, Kevin Kropp, and Ann Marie Glidewell.

Wow, God is so good. From the depths of despair and sadness, to the unbelievable ecstasy of joy and gladness! What a life in Christ!

About the Author

Born in East Providence, Rhode Island, Sharon Garlock Spiegel grew up on the East Coast. The daughter of a pastor. One of seven children, as the only girl for many years, she was dubbed, "Queen of the house". An inquisitive mind and creative imagination, (inherited from her grandmother, Jessie May Garlock), gave birth—at a very young age—to made-up plays and dramas acted out with her siblings.

When her family moved to Springfield, Mo., Sharon enrolled in college—eventually receiving a Bachelor of Science degree in Psychology. She met her husband, Roger while in Springfield, where they both worked at the Assemblies of God International Headquarters. Married 48 years, they have three children, fourteen grandchildren, and one great-grandchild. After marriage she continued her education and earned a Masters Degree in Christian Counseling.

An ordained Assembly of God minister, she is the administrator of a private Christian school and pastor of South Park Assembly of God. In addition she often speaks to groups about her books and her favorite theme: "The Promises of God for Families". Her spare time, (which is rare), includes: writing, reading, spending time with her fourteen grandchildren, traveling with her husband when the opportunity presents itself, (including mission trips).

A Message From the Author

Thank you for taking the time to read my book. I would be honored if you would consider leaving a review for it on **Amazon**.

Author's Note

Our family has been blessed to know the Bill and Deanna Kropp for more than forty years. Bill Kropp and my father, David Garlock, were friends, always trying to out-do each other with humor. More importantly, they served the Lord and each others' ministry, serving on community and ministry projects that have resulted in changed lives. I'll always think of him as "Captain Kropp" because that's the position he held when we first met, although he is now an ordained Assembly of God minister.

It was such a thrill to see them in the congregation the evening I received my ordination with the Assemblies of God. They met me afterward and told me how proud they were of me. It meant a great deal to have them there. My husband Roger and I consider them to be wonderful friends. My father told me once that in life I would meet only a few "Real People." The Kropps are that kind of people.

After my book, *Generations*, was published, I told Bill I wanted to write his story. We would mention it every time we met. Finally I said to him one day, "Bill, you are eighty, I am seventy. If we're going to do this, we need to do it!"

And so here it is. It is an amazing story of

the miracle-working power of God as He changes an individual life, which then affects so many other lives exponentially. What a great God we serve.

The longevity Bill Kropp enjoys is amazing considering the way he abused his body for most of his youth. It is just another of God's bountiful mercies shown as Bill has chosen to follow the leading of God through the power of His Holy Spirit. Eighty years young, he pastors and guides his church through the troubled times in which we live. He has been able by experience and now by example to give wise, prudent counsel and advice as he leads people to follow Christ.

He has the advantage of knowing the depths to which a person can sink if they follow their own way and their own remedy to ease the hurt of loneliness, rejection, and abuse. He followed the way of self-medication through alcohol and total rebellion through criminal activity, but our great and almighty God, who loves beyond measure, reached down and picked him up.

It is amazing to live through his experiences vicariously and comprehend the magnitude of God's work, how God cared enough and kept Deanna from making a horrible mistake. The solution of suicide is NEVER the answer. It just sends waves of grief with unanswered questions that follow loved ones all their lives and robs the one committing the act of living their life, trusting God to bring them to a place of peace and eternal life through Christ. The enemy of our souls works hard to bring a person to the place where they see taking their life or the life of their precious child as the only answer. Driven to the depths of suicidal despair only brings more pain and no answers.

It is a blessing to reflect on how Bill Kropp and my dad, Reverend David Garlock, Sr., became fast friends. They were so much alike in their commitment to serve others, they began to work together on several projects. Aside from their call to ministry, their kindred spirits carried them through difficult times.

Together with a Catholic Nun, Sister Bernice, and local pastors they began a group called *One In the Spirit*. They held services each month in various churches, stressing the work and power of the Holy Spirit in ministry. It drew people from all denominational backgrounds and had an impact on the city of St. Joseph.

Another group they helped to initiate was *Area Ministers for Christ*. Again this organization met with the intent of spreading the Gospel through following Christ's command to love one another. Through this group, a fellowship house was established that ministered to recovering addicts and those coming out of prison and helping them enter society. Biblical principals were taught and emphasized there.

My parents founded a private Christian

school, South Park Christian Academy, in 1976. Bill Kropp helped with encouragement and friendship as the school grew, and continues to encourage and pray for this educational ministry to this day. Through the *Area Ministers for Christ*, another Christian School was founded, St. Joseph Christian School. It is a remarkable school that has grown and ministers to the community. Both South Park Christian Academy and St. Joseph Christian School thrive today because of the vision and cooperative work of men like Bill Kropp, David Garlock, and Joe Gregory.

The West Valley Food Kitchen is another ministry started by the group. Feeding the hungry is one of the outstanding works pinpointed by Jesus in his teaching. The food kitchen is still in operation as a testimony exemplary of the heart of the servants of Christ who founded it. Others continue with the various programs they began, carrying on their vision. These ministries, however, would not exist were it not for the faith and perseverance of these godly men of faith with the courage they exhibited to step out and answer the call of God.

Captain Kropp, now Pastor Kropp, has a true heart after God. He is always the same when your see him, never putting on sanctimonious "airs." He and his wife, Deanna, stand tall in my mind as heroes of the faith—never wavering, but pressing onward and forward as God gives them strength and opportunity.

His testimony of being drawn from what many would consider a miserable beginning in life is amazing. One can see the protective hand of God on him throughout his early days growing up, throughout the war and POW camp, and afterward. Without the encouragement of parents, he has risen from the lowest valley to greatness in the eyes of God, a new creature in Christ, molded and shaped into the man of God he was meant to become. Eighty years young and still going strong, spreading the Gospel and pastoring a growing church, he stands a testimony of God's mercy and grace.

When a story like Bill Kropp's comes to my ears, I am again confounded by the love of God. His love is incomprehensible and beyond our human understanding. The fact that He loves us just the way we are, with all our imperfections and then takes a willing, submissive heart and gives us blessings and favor underserved is beyond amazing. Becoming acquainted with the Kropps before I knew their story, I never would have dreamed of the deep wounds of their past. As I interviewed them and looked back with them at the things they'd been through, we all shed tears. The only scars they seem to have are those hidden under Bill's still thick crop of hair—scars from his adoptive mother's broomstick splitting his skull. But even those are no longer visible, just a light reminder.

Acknowledgements

Thanks and appreciation goes to Bill and Deanna Kropp for allowing me to tell their amazing story. They are two very real and powerful testimonials of God's redeeming, power and the miraculous workings of God in the lives of two humble people with servants' hearts.

I acknowledge too, Amazing Things Press and Julie Casey for their willingness to publish this dynamic story. What an honor it has been to have my brother, David Paul Garlock, Jr., PhD. edit this book. With great appreciation and thanks, I acknowledge the time and expertise he put into this project.

Most of all, praise and Glory is given to the one who rescued Bill from his road to destruction. Through the power of the Cross of Calvary where Christ took on the sins of the world, it is possible for anyone to become changed, a new creature in Christ, Jesus.

Shorty Mills knew the power of John 3:16. He quoted it continually to Bill in that gunner's nest. I urge you, our reader, if you have not yet done so, to acknowledge the wonderful gift of God's Son to make you a new creature in Him. No matter your circumstance, accepting this gift of redemption will take you on a wonderful journey, through a life surrendered to God's Will. There is nothing more fulfilling or satisfying and the result is Everlasting Life in Christ!

Even though born without a paternal family history, Bill Kropp became a child of God and that was his identity. Loved, forgiven, called by His Lord and Savior, Jesus Christ!

Check out these books from
Amazing Things Press

Keeper of the Mountain by Nshan Erganian

Rare Blood Sect by Robert L. Justus

Survival In the Kitchen by Sharon Boyle

Stop Beating the Dead Horse by Julie L. Casey

In Daddy's Hands by Julie L. Casey

MariKay's Rainbow by Marilyn Weimer

Seeking the Green Flash by Lanny Daise

Thought Control by Robert L. Justus

Fun Activities to Help Little Ones Talk by Kathy Blair

Bighorn by James Ozenberger

Post Exodus by Robert Christiansen

Rawnie's Mirage by Marilyn Weimer

All American Prizefighter by Rob Calloway

Fall of Grace by Rachel Riley and Sharon Spiegel

Taming the Whirlwind by Lindsey Heidle

John Henry's War by Larry W. Anderson

The Brothers' Murder by Brenda Grant

A Good Life by Sarah Rowan

Desperate Reunion…the Promise by Marylin & Nshan Erganian

Died Innocent by Don Nothstine

The Thornless Rose: Fire Blush by Samantha Fidler-Newby

Check out these Poetry books/Collections from
Amazing Things Press

Evoloving by James Fly

Starlings by Jeff Foster

Nightmares or Memories by Nona j. Moss

Tales From Beneath the Crypt by Megan Marie

Palightte by James Fly

Vintage Mysteries by Megan Marie

Tears and Prayers by Harold W. "Doc" Arnett

Thoughts of Mine by Thomas Kirschner

Inner Reflections by Shivonne Jean Hancock

Scanner Code by David Noe

Blanc Mange by Jeff Foster

Zenphoniquely by James Fly

Kin by David Noe

Voices in My Pen by David Noe

Thoughts of Mine II by Thomas Kirschner

www.amazingthingspress.com

Made in the USA
San Bernardino, CA
28 January 2017